YES TO LIFE

Viktor E. Frankl, 1946

VIKTOR E. FRANKL

YES TO LIFE

In Spite of Everything

INTRODUCTION BY DANIEL GOLEMAN
AFTERWORD BY FRANZ VESELY

BEACON PRESS, BOSTON

To my late father

CONTENTS

INTRODUCTION

Saying Yes to Life

I T'S A MINOR MIRACLE THIS BOOK EXISTS. THE LECTURES that form the basis of it were given in 1946 by the psychiatrist Viktor Frankl a scant eleven months after he was liberated from a labor camp where, a short time before, he had been on the brink of death. The lectures, edited into a book by Frankl, were first published in German in 1946 by the Vienna publisher Franz Deuticke. The volume went out of print and was largely forgotten until another publisher, Beltz, recovered the book and proposed to republish it. *Yes to Life: In Spite of Everything* has never before been published in English.

During the long years of Nazi occupation, Viktor Frankl's audience for the lectures published in this book had been starved for the moral and intellectual stimulation he offered them and were in dire need of new ethical coordinates. The Holocaust, which saw millions die in concentration camps, included as victims Frankl's parents and his pregnant wife. Yet despite these personal tragedies and the inevitable deep sadness these losses brought Frankl, he was able to put such suffering in a perspective that has inspired millions of readers of his best-known book, *Man's Search for Meaning*—and in these lectures.

He was not alone in the devastating losses and his own near death but also in finding grounds for a hopeful outlook despite it all. The daughter of Holocaust survivors tells me that her parents had a network of friends who, like them, had survived some of the same horrific death camps as Frankl. I had expected her to say that they had a pessimistic, if not entirely depressed, outlook on life.

But, she told me, when she was growing up outside Boston her parents would gather with friends who were also survivors of the death camps—and have a party. The women, as my Russian-born grandmother used to say, would get "gussied up," wearing their finest clothes, decking themselves out as though for a fancy ball. They would gather for lavish feasts, dancing and being merry together—"enjoying the good life every chance they had," as their daughter put it. She remembers her father saying "That's living" at even the slightest pleasures.

As she says, "They never forgot that life was a gift that the Nazi machine did not succeed in taking away from them." They were determined, after all the hells they had endured, to say "Yes!" to life, in spite of everything.

The phrase "yes to life," Viktor Frankl recounts, was from the lyrics of a song sometimes sung *sotto voce* (so as not to anger guards) by inmates of some of the four camps in which he was a prisoner, the notorious Buchenwald among them. The song had bizarre origins. One of the first commanders of Buchenwald—built in 1937 originally to hold political prisoners—ordered that a camp song be written. Prisoners, often already exhausted from a day of hard labor and little food, were forced to sing the song over and over. One camp survivor said of the singing, we "put all our hatred" into the effort.

But for others some of the lyrics expressed hope, particularly this:

> . . . *Whatever our future may hold:*
> *We still want to say "yes" to life,*
> *Because one day the time will come—*
> *Then we will be free!*

If the prisoners of Buchenwald, tortured and worked and starved nearly to death, could find some hope in those lyrics despite their unending suffering, Frankl asks us, shouldn't we, living far more comfortably, be able to say "Yes" to life in spite of everything life brings us?

That life-affirming credo has also become the title of this book, a message Frankl amplified in these talks. The basic themes that he rounded out in his widely read book *Man's Search for Meaning* are hinted at in these lectures given in March and April of 1946, between the time Frankl wrote *Man's Search* and its publication.

For me there is a more personal resonance to the theme of *Yes to Life*. My parents' parents came to America around 1900, fleeing early previews of the intense hatred and brutality that Frankl and other Holocaust survivors endured. Frankl began giving these talks in March of 1946, just around the time I was born, my very existence an expression of my parents' defiance of the bleakness they had just witnessed, a life-affirming response to those same horrors.

In the rearview mirror offered by more than seven decades, the reality Frankl spoke to in these talks has long gone, with successive generational traumas and hopes following one on another. We postwar kids were by and large aware of the horrors of the death camps, while today relatively few young people know the Holocaust occurred.

Even so, Frankl's words, shaped by the trials he had just endured, have a surprising timeliness today.

～

Recognizing a "Big Lie" was a homework assignment in the civics class at my California high school, the Big Lie being a standard ploy in propaganda. For the Nazis, one Big Lie was that so-called Aryans were a supposed "master race," somehow ordained to rule the world. The defeat of the Nazis put that fantasy to rest.

As World War II ended and the specter of the Cold War rose, with it came the threat that Russians, too, would make propaganda a weapon in their arsenal. And, so, high school students of my era learned to spot and counter malicious half-truths.

As an inoculation against lies coming from Russia at the time, we learned to spot the rudiments of such disinformation, the Big Lie among them. Propaganda, as we learned in my civics class, relies on not just lies and misinformation but also on distorted negative stereotypes, inflammatory terms, and other such tricks to manipulate people's opinions and beliefs in the service of some ideological agenda.

Propaganda had played a major role in shaping the outlook of people ruled by the Axis powers. Hitler had argued that people would believe anything if it was repeated often enough and if disconfirming information was routinely denied, silenced, or disputed with yet more lies. Frankl knew well the toxicity of propaganda deployed by the Nazis in their rise to power and beyond. It was aimed, he saw, at the very value of existence itself, asserting the worthlessness of life—at least for anyone, like himself, who fell into a maligned category, like gypsies, gays, Jews, and political dissidents, among others.

When he was imprisoned in Nazi concentration camps, Frankl himself became a victim of such systematic lies, brutalized by guards who saw him and his fellow prisoners as less than human. When he gave the lectures in this book a scant nine months after his liberation from the Turkheim labor camp, Frankl began his talk by decrying the negative propaganda that had destroyed any sense of meaning, human ethics, and the value of life. As he and all those in his Viennese audience knew well, the Nazis had honed their propaganda skills to a high level. But the kind of civics lesson that taught how to spot such distortions of truth is long gone.

Throughout the centuries, as today, the same disinformation playbook has been put to use by authoritarian rulers worldwide. The signs are clear: shutting down opposition media, quashing dissident voices, and jailing journalists who dare to report something other than the prevailing party line. The danger of substituting for real, objective news instead sets of lies, flimsy conspiracy theories, and us-versus-them hatreds has been amplified by digital media, where those who share beliefs in some or another distorted outlook can find online refuge among others whose minds are likewise set in a sympathetic worldview—and encounter no disconfirming evidence. Niche propaganda rules.

I don't recall the specific Big Lie that turned up in my homework. But I can think of several that were revealed in successive decades. One was about smoking. The US government had made a point of giving cigarettes to Allied troops in Europe and Asia—and so hooked a generation on a habit that, in the end, shortened their lives. When I was young, smoking was seen as glamorous (advertising, too, can partake of the Big Lie). Now we know that habit heightens the likelihood of cancer and heart disease, and an earlier death.

Another Big Lie had to do with my local power company, PG&E. When I was young, that utility had the image of being trustworthy. These days we know once that public utility became a private company, greed and the bottom line meant that profits were taken rather than putting money into repairing and maintaining the outfit's infrastructure. And today that once reliable organization has been the cause of countless wildfires—and has gone into bankruptcy.

The kind of lesson I had in spotting propaganda has long since dropped off the school curriculum. Yet it seems the time has again come when simple truths and basic human values need defending against the dangerous tides of hatred-spewing propagandists. Is it time again to bring back civics—lessons in speaking up, being a responsible citizen, and spotting today's Big Lies?

That's happening a bit already: new initiatives all over the country—indeed the world—are working to ensure that middle and high school students are taught lessons in these crucial areas.

In an age when media of every kind have become tools of persuasion and propaganda, these are the kinds of questions any of us might do well to ask.

*

It might seem odd to readers today that Frankl spends a good deal of time refuting the assumption underlying euthanasia—not in its literal meaning, a "good," gentle, and painless death but rather in its perverse sense: that certain lives have no value, including those of the mentally ill and developmentally challenged, and so their deaths are justified.

The Nazis had murdered such people, no doubt a fact quite fresh in Frankl's mind just months after the war ended. As a psychiatrist, Frankl would have been acutely aware of the "euthanasia" policy that killed people like his former charges at the institution where he had worked before the war.

Frankl argues that suffering, even incurable illness and the inner dignity of dying "one's own death," can prove meaningful. In the face of death, for instance, there can still be an inner success, whether in maintaining a certain attitude or given the fulfillment of that person's life's meaning. So, he contends, no one has the right to judge another person's life as meaningless, or to deem another as unworthy of the right to life. Frankl himself had just recently been freed from the camps where the lives of inmates like him "counted for nothing."

While the Holocaust rightly counts as an evil perpetrated on ethnic, political, and religious groups deemed by the Nazis as worthless, the extermination policy was also applied to those with mental handicaps in huge numbers—several hundred thousand by some counts. The approach had, oddly, originated in the American "eugenics" movement, a form of social Darwinism that justified a society in ridding itself of those who were deemed unfit, often through forced sterilization. That argument was carried to its logical, if horrific, fulfillment by the Nazis.

Murdering such people has, blessedly, largely vanished around the globe as a tactic for dealing with those once deemed "undesirable." Today's disputes around euthanasia revolve around the "good death" sense of the term, in which a terminally ill person, typically in great pain, opts for suicide to put an end to their own suffering.

Frankl's main contribution to the world of psychotherapy was what he called "logotherapy," which treats psychological problems by helping people find meaning in their lives. Rather than just seeking happiness, he proposed, we can seek a sense of purpose that life offers us.

Happiness in itself does not qualify as such a purpose; pleasures do not give our life meaning. In contrast, he points out that even the dark and joyless episodes of our lives can be times when we mature and find meaning. He even posits that the more difficult, the more meaningful troubles and challenges can be. How we deal with the tough parts of our lives, he observes, "shows who we are."

If we can't change our fate, at least we can accept it, adapt, and possibly undergo inner growth even in the midst of troubles. This approach was part of a school known as "existential therapy," which addresses the larger issues of life, like dealing with suffering and dying—all of which Frankl argued are better handled when a person has a clear sense of purpose. Existential therapies, including Frankl's version, blossomed particularly as part of the humanistic psychology movement that peaked in the 1970s and continued in successive decades. To be sure, a robust lineage of logotherapy and existential analysis continues to this day.

There are three main ways people find fulfillment of their life meaning, in Frankl's view. First, there is action, such as creating a work, whether art or a labor of love—something that outlasts us and continues to have an impact. Second, he says, meaning can be found in appreciating nature, works of art, or simply loving people; Frankl cites Kierkegaard, that the door to happiness always opens outward. The third lies in how a person adapts and reacts to unavoidable limits on their life possibilities, such as facing their own death or enduring a dreadful fate like the concentration camps. In short, our lives take on meaning through our actions, through loving, and through suffering.

Here I'm reminded of life advice from the Dalai Lama on the occasion of his eightieth birthday, when I wrote *A Force for Good: The Dalai Lama's Vision for Our World*. First, he recommended, gain some internal control over your own mind and how you react to life's difficulties. Then, adopt an ethic of compassion and altruism, the urge to help others. Finally, act on that outlook in whatever ways your life offers.

Frankl cites a converging formulation from Rabbi Hillel almost two thousand years ago. The translation I know best goes: "If I am not for myself, who will be for me? If I am not for others, what am I? And if not now, when?" For Frankl, this suggests that each of us has our unique life purpose and that serving others ennobles it. The scope and range of our actions matter less than how well we respond to the specific demands of our life circle.

A common thread in these disparate words of wisdom comes down to the ways we respond to life's realities moment to moment, in the here and now, as revealing our purpose in an ethics of everyday life. Our lives continually pose the question of our life's meaning, a query we answer by how we respond to life.

To be sure, Frankl saw human frailty, too. Each of us, he notes, is imperfect—but imperfect in our own way. He put a positive spin on this, too, concluding that our unique strengths and weaknesses make each of us uniquely irreplaceable.

⤳

The great majority of those who, like Frankl, were liberated from Nazi concentration camps chose to leave for other countries rather than return to their former homes, where far too many neighbors had turned murderous. But Viktor Frankl chose to stay in his native Vienna after being freed and became head of neurology at a main hospital in Vienna.

The Austrians he lived among often perplexed Frankl by saying they did not know a thing about the horrors of the camps he had barely survived. For Frankl, though, this alibi seemed flimsy. These people, he felt, had *chosen* not to know.

Another survivor of the Nazis, the social psychologist Ervin Staub, was saved from a certain death by Raoul Wallenberg, the diplomat who made Swedish passports for thousands of desperate Hungarians, keeping them safe from the Nazis. Staub studied cruelty and hatred, and he found one of the roots of such evil to be the turning away, choosing not to see or know, of bystanders. That not-knowing was read by perpetrators as a tacit approval. But if instead witnesses spoke up in protest of evil, Staub saw, it made such acts more difficult for the evildoers.

For Frankl, the "not-knowing" he encountered in postwar Vienna was regarding the Nazi death camps scattered throughout that short-lived empire, and the obliviousness of Viennese citizens to the fate of their own neighbors who were imprisoned and died in those camps. The underlying motive for not-knowing, he points out, is to escape any sense of responsibility or guilt for those crimes. People in general, he saw, had been encouraged by their authoritarian rulers not to know—a fact of life today as well.

That same plea of innocence, *I had no idea*, has contemporary resonance in the emergence of an intergenerational tension. Young people around the world are angry at older generations for leaving as a legacy to them a ruined planet, one where the momentum of environmental destruction will go on for decades, if not centuries.

This environmental not-knowing has gone on for centuries, since the Industrial Revolution. Since then we have seen the invention of countless manufacturing platforms and processes, most all of which came to be in an era when we had no idea of their ecological impacts. Advances in science and technology are making ecological impacts more transparent, and so creating options that address the climate crisis and, hopefully, will be pursued across the globe and over generations.

Such disruptive, truly "green" alternatives are one way to lessen the bleakness of Earth 2.0—the planet in future decades—a compelling fact of life for today's young. Were Frankl with us today (he died in 1997), he would no doubt be pleased that so many of today's younger people are choosing to know and are finding purpose and meaning in surfacing environmental facts and acting on them.

In light of the wholesale madness that afflicted too much of the "civilized" world during the great war that had just passed, Frankl felt the younger generation of his day no longer had the kind of role models that would give them a sense of enthusiastic idealism, the energy that drives progress. The young people who had witnessed the war, he felt, had seen too much cruelty, pointless suffering, and devastating loss to harbor a positive outlook, let alone enthusiasm.

The years leading up to and including the war, he noted, had "utterly discredited" all principles, leaving the nihilistic perception that the world itself lacked any substance. Frankl asked how it might be possible to resurrect and sustain concepts like a noble meaning in life, which had been so wantonly demolished by a torrent of lies.

In another timely insight, Frankl saw that a materialistic view, in which people end up mindlessly consuming and fixating on what they can buy next, epitomizes a meaningless life, as he put it, where we are "guzzling away" without any thought of morality. That very eagerness for consumption has become today a dominant worldview, one devoid of any greater meaning or inner purpose.

Add to that the degradation of human dignity created by an economic system that had, in the last few decades before Frankl gave his talks, relegated working men and women into "mere means," degrading them into "tools" of making money for someone else. Frankl saw this as an insult to human dignity, arguing that a person should never become a means to an end.

And then there were the concentration camps, where lives seen only as worthy of death were nevertheless exploited as slave labor to their biological limits. From all that—plus the simple fact of collusion with evil leaders—European countries especially were pervaded by a collective sense of guilt. On top of all this, Frankl was acutely aware as a camp survivor that "the best among us" did not return. That knowledge could easily turn into a crippling "survivor's guilt." Small wonder camp survivors like him had to relearn how to be happy at all.

From all these insults to reach any sense of meaning ensued an inner crisis, as Frankl sensed, one that led to the comfortless worldview of a nihilistic existentialism—think Beckett's bleak postwar play *Waiting for Godot*, an expression of the cynicism and hopelessness of those years. As Frankl put it, "It should not be a surprise if contemporary philosophy perceives the world as though it had no substance."

Fast-forward seven decades or more. These days, various lines of evidence suggest that many young people today are putting their sense of meaning and purpose first—a development Frankl could not have foreseen given the dark lens that the horrors he had just survived gave him. But these days, those who recruit and hire for companies, for instance, report that more than any time in memory the new generation of prospective employees shun working for places whose activities conflict with their personal values.

Frankl's intuitive sense of how purpose matters has been borne out by a large body of research. For instance, having a sense of purpose in life offers a buffer against poor health. People with a life purpose, data shows, tend to live longer. And researchers find that having a purpose numbers among the pillars of well-being.

In Beckett's play, Estragon and Vladimir, the two characters waiting for Godot while trapped in a hopeless eternity, both make clumsy attempts at suicide to escape their senseless predicament. Frankl, in contrast, had founded a successful suicide prevention program in the decade before Nazis sent him to the death camps. In German colleges of those days there had been batches of suicides by young students after they received their scores on the exam that determined what further training they would—or would not—get.

But suicide, Frankl argued, represents the height of meaninglessness. "Suicide," he wrote, "is never able to solve a problem" or to answer the question being asked of us by life. Frankl urged that instead of fixating on and exaggerating the catastrophic life consequence of poor scores, students instead contemplate their larger aspirations for their lives. His program, some sources report, reduced those suicides to zero in one of the first years it ran.

"Whoever has a *why* to live can bear almost any *how*," as the German philosopher Friedrich Nietzsche declared. Frankl takes this maxim as an explanation for the will to survive he noted in some fellow prisoners. Those who found a larger meaning and purpose in their lives, who had a dream of what they could contribute, were, in Frankl's view, more likely to survive than were those who gave up.

One crucial fact mattered here. Despite the cruelty visited on prisoners by the guards, the beatings, torture, and constant threat of death, there was one part of their lives that remained free: their own minds. The hopes, imagination, and dreams of prisoners were up to them, despite their awful circumstances. This inner ability was real human freedom; people are prepared to starve, he saw, "if starvation has a purpose or meaning."

The lesson Frankl drew from this existential fact: our perspective on life's events—what we make of them—matters as much or more than what actually befalls us. "Fate" is what happens to us beyond our control. But we each are responsible for how we relate to those events.

Frankl held these insights on the singular importance of a sense of meaning even before he underwent the horrors of camp life, though his years as a prisoner gave him even deeper conviction. When he was arrested and deported in 1941, he had sewn into the lining of his overcoat the manuscript of a book in which he argued for this view. He had hoped to publish that book one day, though he had to give up the coat—and the unpublished book—on his first day as a prisoner. And his desire to one day publish his views, along with his yearning to see his loved ones once again, gave him a personal purpose that helped keep him afloat.

After the war, and with this optimistic outlook on living still intact despite the brutalities of the camps, Frankl in these lectures called on people to strive toward "a new humanity," even in the face of their losses, heartbreaks, and disenchantments. "What is human," he argued, "is still valid."

Frankl recounts asking his students what they thought gave a sense of purpose to his, Frankl's, own life. One student guessed it exactly: to help other people find their purpose. Frankl ended these lectures—and this book— by saying his entire purpose has been that any of us can say "Yes" to life in spite of everything.

—Daniel Goleman
Boston, Winter 2020

ON THE
MEANING
AND
VALUE
OF LIFE I

T O SPEAK ABOUT THE MEANING AND VALUE OF LIFE MAY seem more necessary today (1946) than ever; the question is only whether and how this is "possible." In some respects it is easier today: we can now speak freely again about so many things—things that are inherently connected with the problem of the meaningfulness of human existence and its value, and with human dignity. However, in other respects, it has become more difficult to speak of meaning, value, and dignity. We must ask ourselves: Can we still use these words so easily today? Has not the very meaning of these words become somehow questionable? Have we not seen, in recent years, too much negative propaganda railing against everything they mean, or once meant?

The propaganda of these last years was a propaganda against all possible meaning and against the questionable value of existence itself! In fact, these years have sought to demonstrate the worthlessness of human life.

Since Kant, European thought has succeeded in making clear statements about the true dignity of human beings: Kant himself, in the second formulation of his categorical imperative, said that everything has its value, but man has his dignity—a human being should never become a means to an end. But already in the *economic system* of the last few decades, most *working people* had been turned into mere means, degraded to become mere tools for economic life. It was no longer work that was the means to an end, a means for life or indeed a food for life—rather it was a man and his life, his vital energy, his "man power," that became this means to an end.

And then came the war—the war in which the man and his life were now even made a means for death. And then there were the concentration camps. In the camps, even the life that was considered worthy only of death was fully exploited to its absolute limit. What a devaluation of life, what a debasement and degradation of humankind! Let us try to imagine—so that we can make a judgment—that a state intends somehow to make use of all the people it has condemned to death, to exploit their capacity for labor right up to the very last moment of their lives—perhaps considering that this would be more sensible than simply killing such people immediately, or even feeding them for the rest of their lives. And were we not told often enough in the concentration camps that we were "not worth the soup," this soup that was doled out to us as the sole meal of the day, and the price of which we had to pay with the toil of digging through the earth? We unworthy wretches even had to accept this undeserved gift of grace in the required manner: as the soup was handed to him, each prisoner had to doff his cap. So, just as our lives were not worth a bowl of soup, our deaths were also of minimal value, not even worth a lead bullet, just some Zyklon B.[1]

Finally, it came to the *mass murders* in mental institutions. Here, it became obvious that any person whose life was no longer "productive," even if only in the most wretched manner, was literally declared to be "unworthy of life."

But, as we said earlier, even "Non-Sense" was propagated at that time. What do we mean by this?

Today, our attitude to life hardly has any room for belief in meaning. We are living in a typical postwar period. Although I am using a somewhat journalistic phrase here, the state of mind and the spiritual condition of an average person today is most accurately described as "spiritually bombed out." This alone would be bad enough, but it is made even worse by the fact that we are overwhelmingly dominated, at the same time, by the feeling that we are yet again living in a kind of prewar period. The invention of the atomic bomb is feeding the fear of a catastrophe on a global scale, and a kind of apocalyptic, "end-of-the-world" mood has taken hold of the last part of the second millennium. We already know such apocalyptic moods from history. They existed at the beginning of the first millennium and at its end. And, famously, in the last century there was a *fin-de-siècle* feeling, and this was not the only one that was defeatist; at the root of all these moods lies fatalism.

However, we cannot move toward any spiritual reconstruction with a sense of fatalism such as this. We first have to overcome it. But in doing so, we ought to take into account that today we cannot, with blithe optimism, just consign to history everything these last years have brought with them. We have become pessimistic. We no longer believe in progress in itself, in the higher evolution of humanity as something that could succeed automatically. The blind belief in automatic progress has become a concern only affecting the *self-satisfied stuffed shirts*—today such a belief would be *reactionary*. Today we know what human beings are capable of. And if there is a fundamental difference between the way people perceived the world around them in the past and the way they perceive it at present, then it is perhaps best identified as follows: in the past, activism was coupled with optimism, while today activism requires pessimism. Because today every impulse for action is generated by the knowledge that there is no form of progress on which we can trustingly rely. If today we cannot sit idly by, it is precisely because each and every one of us determines what and how far something "progresses." In this, we are aware that inner progress is only actually possible for each individual, while mass progress at most consists of technical progress, which only impresses us because we live in a technical age. Our actions can now only arise from our pessimism; we are still only able to seize the opportunities in life from a standpoint of skepticism, while the old optimism would just lull us into complacency and induce fatalism, albeit a rosy fatalism. Give me a sober activism anytime, rather than that rose-tinted fatalism!

How steadfast would a person's belief in the meaningfulness of life have to be, so as not to be shattered by such skepticism. How unconditionally do we have to believe in the meaning and value of human existence, if this belief is able to take up and bear this skepticism and pessimism? And just at a time when all idealism has been so disappointed, and all enthusiasm so abused; but when we cannot do other than appeal to idealism or enthusiasm. But the present generation, the youth of today— and it is in the younger generation that we would most likely find idealism and enthusiasm—no longer has any role models. Too many upheavals had to be witnessed by this one generation, too many external—and in their consequences, internal—breakdowns; far too many for a single generation for us to count on them so unquestioningly to maintain their idealism and enthusiasm.

All the programs, all the slogans and principles have been utterly discredited as a result of these last few years. Nothing was able to survive, so it should not be a surprise if contemporary philosophy perceives the world as though it has no substance. But through this nihilism, through the pessimism and skepticism, through the soberness of a "new objectivity" that is no longer that "new" but has grown old, we must strive toward a new humanity. The past few years have certainly disenchanted us, but they have also shown us that what is human is still valid; they have taught us that it is all a question of the individual human being. After all, in the end, what was left was the human being! Because it was the human being that survived amid all the filth of the recent past. And equally it was the human being that was left in the experiences of the concentration camps. (There was an example of this somewhere in Bavaria in which the camp commander, an SS man, secretly spent money from his own pocket to regularly buy medicines for "his" prisoners from the pharmacy in the nearby Bavarian market town; while in the same camp, the senior camp warden, so himself a prisoner, mistreated the camp inmates in the most appalling way: it all came down to the individual human being!)

What remained was the individual person, the human being—and nothing else. Everything had fallen away from him during those years: money, power, fame; nothing was certain for him anymore: not life, not health, not happiness; all had been called into question for him: vanity, ambition, relationships. Everything was reduced to bare existence. Burnt through with pain, everything that was not essential was melted down—the human being reduced to what he was in the last analysis: either a member of the masses, therefore no one real, so really no one—the anonymous one, a nameless thing (!), that "he" had now become, just a prisoner number; or else he melted right down to his essential self. So, in the end, was there something like a decision that needed to be made? It does not surprise us, because "existence"—to the nakedness and rawness of which the human being was returned—is nothing other than a decision.

However, help was at hand for the human being in making this decision; the critical factor was the existence of others, the being of others, specifically their being role models. This was more fruitful than all that talk and all that writing. Because the fact of being is always more pivotal than the word. And it was necessary, and will always remain so, to ask oneself whether this fact is not far more important than writing books or giving lectures: that each of us actualizes the content in our own act of being. That which is actualized is also much more effective. Words alone are not enough. I was once called upon to attend a woman who had committed suicide. On the wall above her couch, neatly framed, a saying hung on the wall: "Even more powerful than fate is the courage that bears it steadfastly." And this fellow human being had taken her own life right under this motto. Certainly, those exemplary people who can and ought to be effective simply by being, are in the minority. Our pessimism knows this; but that is precisely why the concurrent activism matters, that is precisely what constitutes the tremendous responsibility of the few. An ancient myth tells us that the existence of the world is based on thirty-six truly just people being present in it at all times. Only thirty-six! An infinitesimal minority. And yet they guarantee the continuing moral existence of the whole world. But this story continues: as soon as one of these just individuals is recognized as such and is, so to speak, unmasked by his surroundings, by his fellow human beings, he disappears, he is "withdrawn," and then dies instantly. What is meant by that? We will not be far off the mark if we express it like this: as soon as we notice any pedagogical tendency in a role model, we become resentful; we human beings do not like to be lectured to like children.

What does all this prove? What has come through to us from the past? Two things: everything depends on the individual human being, regardless of how small a number of like-minded people there is, and everything depends on each person, through action and not mere words, creatively making the meaning of life a reality in his or her own being. Therefore, we must counter the negative propaganda of recent times, the propaganda of "Non-Sense," of "Non-Meaning," with another propaganda that must be, firstly, individual and, secondly, active. Only then can it be positive.

So much for our initial question as to whether, and in what sense, and in what spirit, one is still able today to be an advocate for meaning and value in life. But as soon as we speak of the meaning of existence, at that moment it is somehow called into question. Once we ask about it explicitly, it has somehow already been doubted. Doubt about the meaningfulness of human existence can easily lead to despair. We then encounter this despair as the decision to commit suicide.

When we are talking about suicide, we must distinguish between four essential, but essentially different, reasons from which the inner will to commit suicide arises. Firstly, suicide can be a consequence—a consequence not of a primarily mental but of a physical, bodily state. This group includes those cases in which someone experiencing a physically determined change of mental state tries to kill themselves almost as if compelled to do so. Naturally, such cases are excluded at the outset from those considered in today's lecture. Then there are people whose determination to commit suicide feeds on a calculation of its effect on their surroundings: people who want to take revenge on someone for something that has been done to them, and who want their urge for revenge to result in the others in question being weighed down by a guilty conscience for the rest of their lives: they must be made to feel guilty for the suicide's death. These cases must also be eliminated when we consider the meaning of life. Thirdly, there are people whose desire to commit suicide comes from the fact that they simply feel tired, tired of life. But this tiredness is a feeling—and we all know that feelings are not reasons. That someone is tired, feels exhausted, is in itself not a reason for them to stop in their tracks. Rather, everything depends on whether carrying on does actually have meaning, whether that makes it worth overcoming the tiredness. What is needed here is simply an answer to the question of the meaning of life, of continuing to live despite persistent world-weariness. As such, the latter is not a counterargument to living on; this continuing to live, however, will only be possible in the knowledge of life's unconditional meaning.

But in truth, a fourth group of people belong here, those who seek to commit suicide because they just cannot believe in the meaning of living on, in the meaning of life itself. A suicide with that kind of motivation is commonly called a "balance-sheet suicide." In each case it results from a so-called negative life balance. Such a person creates a "balance sheet" and compares what they have (credit) with what they feel they ought to have (debit); they weigh up what life still owes them against what profit they believe they can still derive from life, and the negative balance that they then calculate induces them to commit suicide. We will now set about inspecting this balance sheet.

Normally, the credit column contains all the suffering and pain; the debit column lists all the happiness and good fortune that one did not attain. But this balance is fundamentally incorrect. For, as the saying goes, "We are not in this world for fun." And this is true in the double sense of what is (being) and what ought to be. Anyone who has not felt this for themselves may wish to refer to the writings of a Russian experimental psychologist, who once proved that the average person experiences significantly more feelings of dissatisfaction than feelings of pleasure. Therefore, from the outset, it would not be possible to live only for the sake of pleasure. But is that even necessary—is that what life stands for? Let us imagine a man who has been sentenced to death and, a few hours before his execution, has been told he is free to decide on the menu for his last meal. The guard comes into his cell and asks him what he wants to eat, offers him all kinds of delicacies; but the man rejects all his suggestions. He thinks to himself that it is quite irrelevant whether he stuffs good food into the stomach of his organism or not, as in a few hours it will be a corpse. And even the feelings of pleasure that could still be felt in the organism's cerebral ganglia seem pointless in view of the fact that in two hours they will be destroyed forever.

But the whole of life stands in the face of death, and if this man had been right, then our whole lives would also be meaningless, were we only to strive for pleasure and nothing else—preferably the most pleasure and the highest degree of pleasure possible. Pleasure in itself cannot give our existence meaning; thus the lack of pleasure cannot take away meaning from life, which now seems obvious to us.

A man whose life was saved after a suicide attempt told me one day how he wanted to get out of town to put a bullet through his head, and how, as it was already late in the evening and the trams were no longer running, he felt obliged to take a taxi, and how he found himself fretting about how he did not want to waste money on taxi rides, and how he finally had to smile about the fact that he could have such qualms shortly before his death. It must have seemed pointless to this man who was bent on committing suicide to be stingy about spending money—in the face of death. How beautifully

Rabindranath Tagore expressed all this, the disappointment human beings feel toward their claim to happiness in life, in this poem in which he says:

> *I slept and dreamt*
> *that life was joy.*
> *I awoke and saw*
> *that life was duty.*
> *I worked—and behold,*
> *duty was joy.*

And by this, we are indicating the direction we will take in our further deliberations.

So, life is somehow duty, a single, huge obligation. And there is certainly joy in life too, but it cannot be pursued, cannot be "willed into being" as joy; rather, it must arise spontaneously, and in fact, it does arise spontaneously, just as an outcome may arise: Happiness should not, must not, and can never be a goal, but only an outcome; the outcome of the fulfillment of that which in Tagore's poem is called duty, and that we will later try to define more closely. In any case, all human striving for happiness, in this sense, is doomed to failure as luck can only fall into one's lap but can never be hunted down. It was Kierkegaard who told the wise parable that the door to happiness always opens "outward," which means it closes itself precisely against the person who tries to push the door to happiness "inward," so to speak.

I once had two world-weary people sitting opposite me—as chance would have it, at the same time—a man and a woman. Both had stated, in complete agreement, word for word, that their own lives were meaningless, that they "no longer expected anything of life." Somehow both seemed to be right. It soon emerged, however, that, conversely, something was waiting for each of them: for the man, a scientific work that was unfinished, and for the woman, a child who was living abroad, far away and out of reach. At this point it would be helpful, as we might say with Kant, to "perform a Copernican revolution," a conceptual turn through 180 degrees, after which the question can no longer be *"What can I expect from life?"* but can now only be *"What does life expect of me?"* What task in life is waiting for me?

Now we also understand how, in the final analysis, the question of the meaning of life is not asked in the right way, if asked in the way it is generally asked: it is not we who are permitted to ask about the meaning of life—it is life that asks the questions, directs questions at us—we are the ones who are questioned! We are the ones who must answer, must give answers to the constant, hourly question of life, to the essential "life questions." Living itself means nothing other than being questioned; our whole act of being is nothing more than responding to—of being responsible toward—life. With this mental standpoint nothing can scare us anymore, no future, no apparent lack of a future. Because now the present is everything as it holds the eternally new question of life for us. Now everything depends on what is expected of us. As to what awaits us in the future, we don't need to know that any more than we are able to know it. In this connection, I often tell the following story that appeared in a short newspaper article many years ago: A black man who had been sentenced to life imprisonment was deported to Devil's Island. When the ship, the *Leviathan*, was on the high seas, a fire broke out. Due to the calamitous situation the prisoner was released from his shackles and took part in the rescue work. He saved ten lives. As a result, he was later pardoned. I ask you: if one had asked this man before embarking, in fact on the quay at Marseilles, whether continuing to live could have any kind of meaning for him, he would have had to shake his head: What could possibly be waiting for him? But none of us knows what is waiting for us, what big moment, what unique opportunity for acting in an exceptional way, just like the rescue of ten people by that black man aboard the *Leviathan*.

The question life asks us, and in answering which we can realize the meaning of the present moment, does not only change from hour to hour but also changes from person to person: the question is entirely different in each moment for every individual.

We can, therefore, see how the question as to the meaning of life is posed too simply, unless it is posed with complete specificity, in the concreteness of the here and now. To ask about "the meaning of life" in this way seems just as naive to us as the question of a reporter interviewing a world chess champion and asking, "And now, Master, please tell me: which chess move do you think is the best?" Is there a move, a particular move, that could be good, or even the best, beyond a very specific, concrete game situation, a specific configuration of the pieces?

No less naive was the young man who spoke to me one day, many years ago, as I was about to give a little seminar somewhere on the meaning of life. His words went roughly like this: "Hey Frankl, don't be angry with me, I've been invited to my future in-laws tonight. I really do have to go, and I can't stay for your lecture; please be so kind and tell me quickly, what is the meaning of life?"

Whatever is waiting for us now, this specific "challenge of the hour" may demand an answer in a different sense. First of all, our answer can be an active answer, giving an answer through action, answering specific life questions with a deed that we complete or a work that we create. But here, too, we have a number of things to bear in mind. And what I mean now is perhaps best expressed by referring to a concrete experience: one day, a young man sat in front of me who had just confronted me about the question of the meaning or meaninglessness of life. His argument was as follows: "It's easy for you to talk, you have set up counseling centers, you help people, you straighten people out; but I—who am I, what am I—a tailor's assistant. What can I do, how can I give my life meaning through my actions?" This man had forgotten that it is never a question of where someone is in life or which profession he is in, it is only a matter of how he fills his place, his circle. Whether a life is fulfilled doesn't depend on how great one's range of action is, but rather only on whether the circle is filled out.

In his specific life circle, every single human being is irreplaceable and inimitable, and that is true for everyone. The tasks that his life imposes are only for him, and only he is required to fulfill them. And a person who has not completely filled his (relatively) larger circle remains more unfulfilled than that of a person whose more closely drawn circle is sufficient. In his specific environment, this tailor's assistant can achieve more, and, in the things he does and the things he leaves undone, he can lead a more meaningful life than the person he envies, as long as that person is not aware of his greater responsibility in life and does not do justice to it.

"So, how about *the unemployed?*," you may now object, overlooking the fact that work is not the only field in which we can actively give meaning to our lives. Does work alone make life meaningful? Let's ask the many people who complain to us (not without reason) about how meaningless their (often mechanical) work is, the endless adding up of columns of numbers or the monotonous pushing and pulling of machine levers on *a never-ending production line*. These people can only make their lives meaningful in their all too scant spare time, filling it with personal human meaning. On the other hand, the unemployed person, who has an abundance of free time, also has the chance to endow their life with meaning. No one should believe that we are so frivolous as to underestimate economic difficulties, an economically desperate situation, or, in fact, the sociological or economic factors in such contexts. We know today more than ever, how far "First the grub, then the morals"[2] can take us. We have no illusions about that anymore. But we know how meaningless it is to guzzle away without any morality and how catastrophic this meaninglessness can be to anyone who is fixated only on consumption. And, lastly, we know how much "morality" means: the unshakeable belief in an unconditional meaning to life that, one way or another, makes life bearable. Because we have experienced the reality that human beings are truly prepared to starve if starvation has a purpose or meaning.

However, we have not only witnessed how hard it is to starve if one has no "morality," but we have also seen how hard it is to demand morality from a human being if one lets him starve. Once I had to give the court a psychiatric report on an adolescent boy, who—in the midst of an extremely desperate situation—had stolen a loaf of bread; the court concerned had asked the precise question of whether the boy was "inferior" or not. In my report I had to admit that, from a psychiatric point of view, he could not be considered inferior in any way. But I did not do this without, at the same time, explaining that in his specific situation he would have had to have been "superior" in order to withstand temptation in the face of such hunger!

It is not only through our actions that we can give life meaning—insofar as we can answer life's specific questions responsibly—we can fulfill the demands of existence not only as active agents but also as loving human beings: in our loving dedication to the beautiful, the great, the good. Should I perhaps try to explain for you with some hackneyed phrase how and why experiencing beauty can make life meaningful? I prefer to confine myself to the following thought experiment: imagine that you are sitting in a concert hall and listening to your favorite symphony, and your favorite bars of the symphony resound in your ears, and you are so moved by the music that it sends shivers down your spine; and now imagine that it would be possible (something that is psychologically so impossible) for someone to ask you in this moment whether your life has meaning. I believe you would agree with me if I declared that in this case you would only be able to give one answer, and it would go something like: "It would have been worth it to have lived for this moment alone!"

Those who experience, not the arts, but nature, may have a similar response, and also those who experience another human being. Do we not know the feeling that overtakes us when we are in the presence of a particular person and, roughly translates as, The fact that this person exists in the world at all, this alone makes this world, and a life in it, meaningful.

We give life meaning not only through our actions but also through loving and, finally, through suffering.

Because how human beings deal with the limitation of their possibilities regarding how it affects their actions and their ability to love, how they behave under these restrictions—the way in which they accept their suffering under such restrictions—in all of this they still remain capable of fulfilling human values.

So, how we deal with difficulties truly shows who we are, and that, too, can enable us to live meaningfully. And we should not forget the sporting spirit, that uniquely human spirit! What do athletes do but create difficulties for themselves so that they can grow through overcoming them? In general, of course, it is not advisable to create difficulties for oneself; in general, suffering as a result of misfortune is only meaningful if this misfortune has come about through fate, and is thus unavoidable and inescapable.

Fate, in other words, what happens to us, can certainly be shaped, in one way or another. "There is no predicament which cannot be ennobled either by an achievement or by endurance," said Goethe.[3] *Either we change our fate, if possible, or we willingly accept it, if necessary.* In either case we can experience nothing but inner growth through such misfortune. And now we also understand what Hölderlin means when he writes: "If I step onto my misfortune, I stand higher."[4]

How misguided it now seems to us when people simply complain about their misfortune or rail against their fate. What would have become of each of us without our fate? How else would our existence have taken shape and form than under its hammer blows and in the white heat of our suffering at its hands? Those who rebel against their fate—that is, against circumstances they cannot help and *which they certainly cannot change*—have not grasped the meaning of fate. Fate really is integral in the totality of our lives; and not even the smallest part of what is destined can be broken away from this totality without destroying the whole, the configuration of our existence.

So, fate is part of our lives and so is suffering; therefore, if life has meaning, suffering also has meaning. Consequently, suffering, as long as it is necessary and unavoidable, also holds the possibility of being meaningful. It is actually universally recognized and appreciated as such. Several years ago, the news reached us that the English boy scouts' organization had given awards to three boys for their greatest achievements; and who received these awards? Three boys who were terminally ill in the hospital and who nevertheless endured their burdensome fate with bravery and dignity. This was a clear acknowledgment that true suffering of an authentic fate is an achievement, and, indeed, is the highest possible achievement. The alternative given in the Goethe sentence quoted above is therefore no longer entirely true when examined more closely: in the final analysis, it is not a question of either achievement or endurance—rather, in some cases, endurance itself is the greatest achievement.

The essence of achievement in true suffering, in my opinion, has perhaps been expressed most clearly in

Rilke's words, who once cried out: "How much we must suffer through!" The German language only knows the term "work through." But Rilke grasped that our meaningful achievements in life can be fulfilled at least as well in suffering as in working.

One way or another, there can only be one alternative at a time to give meaning to life, meaning to the moment—so at any time we only need to make one decision about how we must answer, but, each time, a very specific question is being asked of us by life. From all this follows that life always offers us a possibility for the fulfillment of meaning, therefore there is always the option that it has a meaning. One could also say that our human existence can be made meaningful "to the very last breath"; as long as we have breath, as long as we are still conscious, we are each responsible for answering life's questions. This should not surprise us once we recall the great fundamental truth of being human—being human is nothing other than being conscious and being responsible!

But if life always has meaning in accordance with the possibilities, if it only depends on us whether it is filled in every instant with this possible, ever-changing, meaning, if it is entirely our responsibility and our decision to actualize this meaning, then we also know one thing for certain: the one thing that is certainly senseless and has absolutely no meaning is . . . to throw away your life. Suicide is in no way the answer to any question; suicide is never able to solve a problem.

Earlier, we needed to use the game of chess as an allegory for the position of the human being in existence, for his always being confronted by the questions of life; with our example of the "best chess move," we wanted to show how the question of life can only be thought of as a concrete, specific one: as a single question that relates to one person and one situation, one particular person and one particular moment—one question in the here and now. So, once again, we must take the game of chess as an allegory, now when we must show how completely absurd it is to attempt to "solve" a life problem by committing suicide.

Let us imagine for a moment: A chess player is faced with a chess problem and he cannot find the solution, so—what does he do?—he hurls the pieces off the board. Is that a solution to the chess problem? Certainly not.

But this is exactly how the suicide behaves: he throws his life away and thinks he has thereby found a solution for a seemingly insoluble life problem. He does not know that in doing so he has flouted the rules of life— just as the chess player in our allegory has disregarded the rules of the game of chess, within which a chess problem might be solved by moving a knight, castling, or God knows what, at least by a simple chess move, but certainly not by the behavior described. Now, *the suicide also flouts the rules of the game of life; these rules do not require us to win at all costs, but they do demand from us that we never give up the fight.*

Perhaps someone will now object, they admit that "the suicide's behavior goes against all reason; but does not life itself become meaningless in the face of the death that inevitably comes to every human being in the end? Does death not make all our beginnings seem pointless from the start, since nothing endures?" Let us try to find the answer to this objection by asking the question the other way around; let us ask ourselves, "What if we were immortal?" And we can give the answer: if we were immortal, then we could postpone everything, but truly everything. Because it would never matter whether we did a particular thing right now, or tomorrow, or the day after, or in a year, or in ten years, or whenever. No death, no end would be looming over us, there would be no limitation of our possibilities, we would see no reason to do a particular thing right now, or surrender ourselves to an experience just now—there would be time, we would have time, an infinite amount of time.

Conversely, the fact, and only the fact, that we are mortal, that our lives are finite, that our time is restricted and our possibilities are limited, this fact is what makes it meaningful to do something, to exploit a possibility and make it become a reality, to fulfill it, to use our time and occupy it. Death gives us a compulsion to do so. Therefore, death forms the background against which our act of being becomes a responsibility.

If we look at things that way then, essentially, it may prove to be quite irrelevant to us how long a human life lasts. Its long duration does not automatically make it meaningful, and its possible briefness makes it far from meaningless. We also do not judge the life history of a particular person by the number of pages in the book that portrays it but only by the richness of the content it contains.

And there is another question we should address on this occasion: the question of whether the life of a person who has not produced offspring may become meaningless by that very fact alone. We can answer: either a life, an individual life, has meaning, and it must also keep its meaning, if it is not reproduced, if it does not engage in this—we can say, highly illusory—biological "immortalization"; or this individual life, the life of an individual person, does not have a meaning—then it could never acquire meaning merely by seeking to "immortalize" itself by procreation. Because immortalizing something that is inherently "meaningless" is itself meaningless.

From this we can see just one thing: death is a meaningful part of life, just like human suffering. Both do not rob the existence of human beings of meaning but make it meaningful in the first place. Thus, it is precisely the uniqueness of our existence in the world, the irretrievability of our lifetime, the irrevocability of everything with which we fill it—or leave unfulfilled—that gives our existence significance. But it is not only the uniqueness of an individual life as a whole that gives it importance, it is also the uniqueness of every day, every hour, every moment that represents something that loads our existence with the weight of a terrible and yet so beautiful responsibility! Any hour whose demands we do not fulfill, or fulfill halfheartedly, this hour is forfeited, forfeited "for all eternity." Conversely, what we achieve by seizing the moment is, once and for all, rescued into reality, into a reality in which it is only apparently "canceled out" by becoming the past. In truth, it has actually been preserved, in the sense of being kept safe. Having been is in this sense perhaps even the safest form of being. The "being," the reality that we have rescued into the past in this way, can no longer be harmed by transitoriness.

Certainly, our life, in terms of the biological, the physical, is transitory in nature. Nothing of it survives—and yet how much remains! What remains of it, what will remain of us, what can outlast us, is what we have achieved during our existence that continues to have an effect, transcending us and extending beyond us. The effectiveness of our life becomes incorporeal and in that way it resembles radium, whose physical form is also, during the course of its "lifetime" (and radioactive materials are known to have a limited lifetime) increasingly converted into radiation energy, never to return to materiality. What we "radiate" into the world, the "waves" that emanate from our being, that is what will remain of us when our being itself has long since passed away.

There is a simple way, one would almost say a trick, to demonstrate the full extent of the responsibility with which our existence is so poignantly loaded, a responsibility that we can only face trembling, but ultimately somehow joyfully. For there is a kind of categorical imperative that is also a formula of "acting as if," formally similar to Kant's well-known maxim, which goes like this: *"Live as if you were living for the second time and as if you had acted the first time as wrongly as you are about to act now!"*

The essentially finite nature of our existence in time, apparently in the face of death, even though death may be in the distant future, is not the only thing that makes our existence meaningful: the finite nature of our relationship with another person also makes the life of each individual not meaningless but only meaningful. What is meant by this is the fact of our imperfection, our inner limitations, as they can be seen in the different characteristics of human beings. But before we think about the meaningfulness of our imperfection, we must, for the moment, ask whether the despair of human beings over their own imperfection and inadequacy can ever justifiably exist. For we must ask whether people who measure their "being" against a "what ought to be," who thus measure themselves against an ideal, can ever be completely worthless. Is it not rather the case that precisely the fact that they can despair of themselves somehow vindicates them and ultimately, to a certain degree, deprives their despair of legitimacy? Could such people even sit in judgment of themselves if they were so worthless that they were not even able to see the ideal? Does not the distance from the ideal, as soon as they perceive it, confirm that they have not become completely disloyal to this ideal?

And now to the question of the meaning of our imperfections and of our particular imbalances: Let us not forget that each individual person is imperfect, but each is imperfect in a different way, each "in his own way." And as imperfect as he is, he is uniquely imperfect. So, expressed in a positive way, he becomes somehow irreplaceable, unable to be represented by anyone else, unexchangeable. To demonstrate this, we have an apt model from the biological world: originally, in the evolution of living beings, cells are known to have been capable of anything. A "primitive" cell can do anything: it can feed, move, reproduce, and somehow "sense" its environment, etc., and the individual cell only becomes specialized following the slow process of evolution of cells into higher forms of organic cell groups so that the individual cell is finally used only for one single function. According to the principle of progressive division of labor within the whole organism, at the expense of the generally applicable nature of its capabilities, the cell has acquired relative functional irreplaceability. So, for example, a cell from the retina of the eye can no longer feed, no longer move around, and no longer reproduce, but the one thing it can do—i.e., see—it can do exceptionally well. It has therefore become irreplaceable in its specific function. It can no longer be replaced by a skin cell, a muscle cell, or a gamete.

As discussed earlier, just as death proved to be necessary for finding meaning in that it justified the *uniqueness of our existence* and with it our responsibleness, we can now see that the imperfect nature of human beings is meaningful since—now regarded positively—it represents the *individuality of our essential inner being.* However, this uniqueness as a positive value cannot be based on itself alone. Analogous to the functional value of the single cell for the whole organism, the unique individuality of each human being is given value through its relationship with an overarching whole; namely, a human community. Individuality can only be valuable when it is not individuality for its own sake but individuality for the human community. The simple fact that every human being has completely unique ridge patterns on their fingertips is, at most, relevant only to criminologists for crime research or the investigation of a particular criminal; but this biological "individuality" of every human being does not automatically turn the person into a personality or a living being that in its uniqueness is valuable for society.

If we were to try to summarize in a formula the unique nature of existence and the uniqueness of every human being, and this uniqueness as a uniqueness "for"—in other words a uniqueness that is focused on others, on the community—a formula that can remind us of the terrible and glorious responsibility of human beings for the seriousness of their lives, then we could rely on a dictum that Hillel, a founder of the Talmud, made into his motto almost two thousand years ago. This motto is: "If I do not do it, who else will do it? But if I only do it for me, what am I then? And if I do not do it now, then when will I do it?" "If not I"—therein lies the uniqueness of every single person; "If only for me," therein lies the worthlessness and meaninglessness of such uniqueness unless it is a "serving" uniqueness; "and if not now," therein lies the uniqueness of every individual situation!

If we now summarize what we said about the "meaning" of life, we can conclude: life itself means being questioned, means answering; each person must be responsible for their own existence. Life no longer appears to us as a given, but as something given over to us, it is a task in every moment. This therefore means that it can only become more meaningful the more difficult it becomes. The athlete, the climber who actively *seeks* tasks, even creates the difficulties for himself: how delighted is that climber when he finds in a rock face another difficult, an even more difficult, "variant" of his task! At this point we must note, however, that religious people, in their sense of life, in their "understanding of being," distinguish themselves in that they go a step further than the person who merely understands their life as a task, in that they also experience the agency that "gives" them the task or that sets them before the task—the divine being! In other words, religious people experience their life as a divine mission.

And to sum up, what could we say about the question of the "value" of life? The view that presented itself to us is perhaps most aptly expressed in the words of Hebbel, who says: "Life is not something, it is the opportunity for something!"[5]

ON THE
MEANING
AND
VALUE
OF LIFE II

ONE OF THE CONCLUSIONS WE WERE TRYING TO REACH in our first discussion is as follows: if life has a meaning, then suffering must also have a meaning.

Of course, illness is part of suffering. "Part of," we say, because "suffering" and "illness" are not the same thing. A person can suffer without being ill, and they can be ill without suffering. Suffering is such a purely human matter, which in itself is somehow already part of human life, that in some circumstances it is precisely this "nonsuffering" that can actually be an illness. We can observe this particularly in the case of those conditions that are commonly referred to as "mental illnesses" and yet are nothing less than illnesses *of* the mind. For the mind cannot actually get sick; the cognitive dimension can only be true or false, valid or invalid, but never sick. The only thing that can become sick, that can fall ill, is the psyche. However, in such illnesses of the psyche, and particularly in those that are not caused by the psyche itself but are ultimately induced by the physical, in other words the so-called mental illnesses (psychoses, in contrast to the psychologically caused neuroses): many of these cases demonstrate that the inability to suffer becomes a symptom in itself.

A person who has had a syphilitic infection is to some extent threatened, with a certain small percentage of probability, years or decades later, by a syphilitic disease of the brain, called "general paralysis."[6] If he is not aware that, by examining his spinal fluid at certain times or at certain intervals, doctors can accurately and reliably determine whether or not he belongs to this threatened group, he will fear the onset of this mental disorder. (Incidentally, in cases in which the spinal fluid tests positive, malaria treatment can prevent such paralysis, and paralysis that has already developed can be cured by early stage treatment of this type.) This fear of paralysis can itself assume pathological dimensions; in other words, it can be exaggerated into the pathological, the neurotic. But what do we observe if such a person does actually fall ill with general paralysis, and if the (pathologically) feared illness, in fact, occurs? At that moment, he stops being afraid of the illness! And why? Because the symptoms of general paralysis include putting the affected person in a contented mood, due to which he cannot suffer.

A doctor will normally take care not to declare in front of a patient, or even to him, a diagnosis of such a universally dreaded, severe disease as general paralysis. Only in the case of a person suffering from general paralysis are these concerns unfounded. The doctor can candidly explain the exact nature of the disease to such a patient: he will smile and state that the diagnosis is incorrect; and if the doctor were then to point out that the patient is not even able to speak properly, the latter would remain quite unruffled and, as usually happens in such cases, would blame his speech disorder on his bad teeth or his dentures.

Anything that would impress or upset a normal person goes over the head of someone whose ability to suffer has been impaired by a psychological illness, without moving him or having any effect on him at all. Let us take the case of admission to a mental institution, for example. I remember one paralysis sufferer who came into the room in which the institution's doctors first examined newly admitted patients: with a jovial smile and in a decidedly happy mood, he greeted us with words that described how very glad he was to be with us. And while he was later being prepared for a lumbar puncture, he did not show any fear at all and only said: "Of course, I know why you are doing all this to me: to stop me getting bored." And when the puncture was finally performed, during which, after all, he must have felt a stinging sensation, he did, in fact, utter a pensive "Ow!," but not without immediately adding: "Wasn't that splendid?"

If you ignore the fact that the psychically ill person, especially the person who is ill in the sense of "mental illness," has lost the normal capacity for suffering, then what happened to me one day may happen to you. I was on admissions duty in a psychiatric hospital and was called to a newly admitted patient in the admissions hall. When I got there, I found one older and one younger woman, obviously mother and daughter. The mother was behaving in a highly agitated way and wailed about how terrible it all was, while the daughter was trying to calm and console her mother by insisting that everything would be alright, etc. When I needed to address a question to the patient and turned to the distressed mother, the woman pointed her finger behind her daughter's back—that was the patient! The patient herself was not at all upset and was not particularly alarmed at being admitted to a "lunatic asylum": because of her illness she reacted to this certainly not everyday and assuredly less-than-pleasant situation with relative apathy. It is the case that the abnormal reaction (agitated, emotional) to an abnormal situation represents normal behavior. But there are also mental illnesses that cause the patient to—paradoxically as it were—suffer from not being able to suffer! There is, in fact, a special form of melancholy that, unlike the usual form, does not occur alongside depression in the sense of sadness or anxiety; rather, patients complain only that they cannot be happy nor can they suffer, that they are not capable of any emotion at all, whether in relation to pleasant or unpleasant experiences, that their moods are dulled and they feel emotionally cold. Indeed, these patients complain that they cannot even cry, and the despondency of these people just because they are unable to experience suffering is one of the most dreadful forms of despair the psychiatrist can ever witness. How deeply in the consciousness of humankind must lie the knowledge that suffering belongs to life itself!

But for all of us, this fact is not as strange as it would first appear; in our normal spiritual lives, people usually know the extent to which any suffering actually belongs to life. For, let us ask ourselves, honestly and seriously, whether we would want to erase the sad experiences from our past, perhaps from our love lives, whether we would want to miss out on everything that was painful or pain inducing—then we would surely all say no. Somehow we know how much we were able to grow and mature precisely during these joyless periods of our existence.

Now, some of you may object that this has been a deceitful sophistry, more or less a demagogic maneuver on my part, and I should perhaps ask someone who is still in the midst of their suffering—I should ask if they would agree that they willingly accept their suffering! Well, for this purpose, we can draw on experiences, direct, vivid experiences: Not much more than a year ago the men from the concentration camps stood in the ditches and toiled and shoveled and hacked at the icy ground with their picks, so that the sparks flew. And if the guard walked some distance away from the group and if, after a while of not being watched, the shovels and pickaxes rested in their tired hands, conversations began among the men out there in the work detachment and these conversations at the work site, they were always the same, revolving with repetitive monotony of spirit around the same topic: grub. Recipes were exchanged and menus planned, and one man would ask the other about his favorite dish or would rave about various delicacies, and they imagined what they would serve each other someday, when, after their liberation from the camp, they invited one another to dinner. But the best among them did not wish for this day of liberation so that they could once again indulge in culinary delights, but for a completely different reason: so that finally this whole subhuman situation, in which you were compelled to think of nothing but filling your belly, could come to an end; this state in which you cannot think about anything else apart from whether it is already quarter or half past nine in the morning or half-past eleven or quarter to twelve (noon), and how many more hours will pass in this freezing ditch, with this empty stomach until the brief lunch break, or until evening when you can start the march back to the camp to finally get your hands on that bowl of soup in the kitchen. How we longed for proper human suffering at that time, real human problems, real human conflicts, in place of these degrading questions of eating or starving, freezing or sleeping, toiling or being beaten. With deep melancholy and sadness we thought back to the time when we still had our human sufferings, problems, and conflicts and not the suffering and perils of an animal; but when thinking ahead to the future, how heartfelt was our longing for a state in which we would exist by no means without suffering, problems, and conflicts, in which we would indeed have

to suffer, but to suffer that particular form of meaningful suffering that has been imposed on a human being in
his very humanity.

We have already heard that the fulfillment of meaning
is possible in three main directions: human beings are
able to give meaning to their existence, firstly, by doing
something, by acting, by creating—by bringing a work
into being; secondly, by experiencing something—nature, art—or loving people; and thirdly, human beings are
able to find meaning even where finding value in life is not
possible for them in either the first or the second way—
namely, precisely when they take a stance toward the unalterable, fated, inevitable, and unavoidable limitation of
their possibilities: how they adapt to this limitation, react
toward it, how they accept this fate. In the course of life,
human beings must be prepared to change the direction
of this fulfillment of meaning, often abruptly, according
to the particular "challenges of the hour." For we have already pointed out that the meaning of life can only be a
specific one, specific both in relation to each individual
person and in relation to each individual hour: the question that life asks us changes both from person to person,
and from situation to situation. At this point I would like
to show, with an example, how this change of direction
could both be "demanded" by fate and completed "obe-
diently" by the person in question.

There was a young man engaged in an active and productive career—he was a busy graphic designer in advertising—who was suddenly torn from his work because

he fell ill with a malignant, inoperable spinal cord tumor at the top of his spine. This tumor quickly caused paralysis of his arms and legs. Now he could no longer keep up the way in which he had made his life meaningful, namely the path of being active and employed: he was pushed to one side, in a completely different direction; being active was becoming increasingly inaccessible, and he was relying ever more on finding meaning in the passive experiences of his restricted situation, and extracting meaning from life even within such limited possibilities. So, what did our patient do? While he was in the hospital, he read intensively, he tackled books he had never had time to read in his busy professional life, he listened diligently to music on the radio and had the most stimulating discussions with individual fellow patients. So he had withdrawn into that area of existence in which it is possible, beyond being active, for a person to fulfill the meaning of life and answer life's question in the passive incorporation of the world into the self. Therefore, it is understandable that this brave person, even at that point, by no means had the feeling that his life, even in its very limited form, had become meaningless. But then came the time when his illness was so advanced that his hands could no longer hold a book, his muscles had become so weak; he could no longer tolerate headphones as they caused him such severe headaches; and eventually he found it difficult to speak, and could no longer hold his spirited discussions with the other patients. Thus, this man was again pushed to one side, rejected by fate, but now not only from the realm of value creation but also from that of experiential value. Due to his illness, this was the situation in his last days. But he was able to extract meaning even from this state of affairs, simply in the position he adopted. Our patient knew perfectly well that his days, or even hours, were numbered. I remember clearly making my rounds as the doctor on duty at the hospital at the time, on this man's last afternoon. As I was passing his bed, he beckoned to me. Speaking with difficulty, he told me that during the senior physician's rounds that morning he had over-heard that Professor G. had given orders to give the patient a morphine injection in his last few hours, to ease the agony of his impending death throes. He went on to say that since he now had reason to believe that tonight he would reach that point, he asked me to give him the injection now, during that visit, so that the night nurse would not have to call me especially because of him and disturb me while I was sleeping. In the last hours of his life this man was still intent on sparing others trouble rather than "disturbing" them! Apart from the bravery with which he endured all his suffering and pain, what an achievement, not a professional but an unparalleled human achievement, lies in this simple remark, in this wish to consider others, literally in his last hour!

You will understand me if I now state that no terrific advertising graphics, not the best nor the most beautiful in the world (if the patient had created them when he was professionally employed) would have been an accomplishment equal to the simple human achievement that this man demonstrated with his behavior in those last few hours of his life.

So we can see that illness does not necessarily involve a loss of meaning, an impoverishment in meaning of our existence; but depending on the possibilities, it is always something meaningful. That a loss of meaning does not necessarily have to occur, even where a person suffers a physical loss to his body, is demonstrated by the following case: One day, one of the most respected judges in Austria was brought to a hospital where I was working. Arteriosclerosis had caused a chronic inflammation and the patient had to have one of his legs amputated. Having survived the operation well, the day came for him to attempt his first one-legged steps. He climbed out of bed with my assistance and began laboriously and forlornly hopping around the room on one leg, like a sparrow. Then he suddenly burst into tears, and the venerable, world-famous old man whose hands I was holding wept softly like a little child: "I can't stand it, there is no point in living life as a cripple," he whimpered. Then I looked him in the eye and asked him insistently, but facetiously: "Tell me, Your Honor, do you intend to pursue a successful career as a short- or long-distance runner?" He looked up, astonished. "Because then," I continued, "but only then, would I be able to understand your despair and your previous statement; because then you would have played your last card, for then your further life, your living on, would be pointless for you: because you would no longer be capable of being a short- or a long-distance runner. But beyond that, for a man like you who has led his whole life in a highly meaningful way, who has been effective and made a name for himself in the professional world—for such a man, should the whole of life have lost its meaning just because he has lost a leg?" The man immediately understood what I meant, and a smile broke out across his tear-stained face.

So, illness does not have to lead to a loss of meaning. But more than that, sometimes it can even lead to a benefit. In order to make this possibility clear for you I would like to tell you about a case that occurred in a concentration camp. There, I once met a woman of younger years who I had known before. When I saw her again in the camp she was in a terrible state and mortally ill—and knew it. But a few days before she died, she said: "I am grateful to fate for bringing me here; in my earlier, bourgeois life I aspired to be cultured, but somehow I was not very serious about it. But now I am happy, despite everything. Now everything has become serious and I can, I must, prove myself." As she said this, she was more cheerful than I had ever known her. In this way she was fortunate, she had succeeded in doing what Rilke demanded of every human being or wished for every human being: "to be able to die his own death".[7] In other words, to meaningfully incorporate even death into the whole of life, yes, even to fulfill the meaning of life in death.

Therefore, we no longer need to feel surprised if there are people who (acknowledging the meaningfulness of death within the total meaning of life) see no loss in illness and death and see not only a gain but almost a "gift." An original letter lies in front of me, a letter that, I would like to stress, was not written to me, so that the writer certainly could not have guessed that I would ever use his words as an example in a lecture. But before I read out the relevant passages from the letter I would like to give you the background to the story. This man was quite suddenly struck down by a severe and life-threatening disease of the spinal cord. In order to receive better care, he stayed at the country house of a female friend some distance away from Vienna. Friends had consulted one of the most famous European specialists, and he had been negative about the possibility of surgery for the patient. Even an operation, he had maintained, would have, at most, a 5 percent chance of success. All this was reported by another of the friends in a letter to the lady of the house whose guest my patient was. This letter was brought into the room on a tray by the unwitting chamber maid while the hostess and her sick guest were breakfasting together. And so, in the patient's letter that I hold in my hands, he describes all this and then continues:

> So it was unavoidable for . . . to allow me to get sight
> of the letter from . . . otherwise she would have had
> to break a longstanding habit, and I would have been
> able to draw my own conclusions anyway. (One day,
> I was urged by a friend, if I remember correctly, to go

with him to see the first talking movie that was playing in . . . *Titanic*.[8] With his masterful portrayal, Fritz Kortner played the paralyzed poet in the wheelchair, who, after futile resistance, lets the water rise up around him and then, intoning the Lord's Prayer, firmly and resolutely leads a small group to their fateful deaths. I came out of this first cinematic experience completely shaken and thought that it must be a gift of fate to approach death so resolutely. Now I have been granted this for my own death! I can once again put to the test my fighting spirit; but, from the outset, this fight is not about victory but a final gathering of my strength, so to speak, like one last gymnastic exercise. I want to endure the pain without narcotics as long as I possibly can. "Fighting a losing battle" . . . this expression cannot be allowed to exist within our worldview! It's only about fighting.) After reading the letter from . . . with the opinion of professor . . . we played Bruckner's "Fourth," the Romantic Symphony, in the evening. Everything in me was full of flowing, soothing space. By the way, I'm doing mathematics every day and I don't feel at all sentimental. All the best, your . . .

At this point, none of you can reproach me any longer and suggest that it was easy for me to talk, but you would like to see a patient who really holds to their attitude in the face of death, in the manner in which I presented it as possible and therefore as necessary: it was not easy for the writer of that letter to talk, and yet he acted and thereby showed that what is demanded can also be realized.

It will now be clear to you that the meaning that can ensue from illness and dying cannot be affected by any external lack of success or any failure in this world, that this is rather an internal success, and this inner success exists despite external failure. What may also be clear is perhaps that all this is not only true for special cases, but we can apply it to all our lives and the whole of our lives. For somehow all our lives are ultimately unsuccessful, to the extent that we understand success as only being external success: no external success, no effect, that is to say, no biological or sociological influence out there in the world, is guaranteed to outlive us or even to last forever. However, inner success, the inner fulfillment of life's meaning, is something that, if at all, has been achieved "once and for always." The fact that this goal is often only reached at the end of our existence does not detract from the meaning of life but rounds off this "end" to become a true completion. It is hard to make these things visible and believable using everyday examples. Art offers us more opportunities in this regard. For example, I would like you to remind you of the novella by Werfel, *The Man Who Conquered Death* (*Der Tod des Kleinbürgers*). Werfel describes the figure of the everyday, small, petty bourgeois man, whose entire life consists of misery and worry and seems to be absorbed by it. This man falls ill and is taken to the hospital. And now Werfel shows us how the man leads a heroic fight against his approaching death, because his family would receive an insurance premium if he only dies after New Year's Day, but otherwise no claim could be made on the insurance. And in this fight against death, in this striving to experience New Year's Day, in this struggle for the financial security of his family, this plain and simple man takes on a human greatness that only a poet can portray. Or think of the more or less parallel event in the novel *The Death of Ivan Ilyich*, by Tolstoy. Here, too, we are dealing with a petty bourgeois man who at first despairs when facing death and the unfathomable meaninglessness of his previous existence as he now perceives it, but in his despair over this meaninglessness, he changes, and in this change, with this change, he somehow retrospectively gives his futile life meaning; in fact, it is precisely through this experience of past futility that he dedicates his life as a whole to being meaningful.

If, after all this, it has been proven that even an ailing life, indeed even a life at death's door, is by no means a meaningless life, then we must now turn to the question of what right anyone could ever have to assert that a sick or moribund person, a "terminally ill" person, is a worthless person, that their life is thus "unworthy of life." Here, we want to disregard any practical value, that is, any usefulness that the lives of sick individuals could have, indeed precisely their lives, insofar as they can contribute to the discovery of new diseases or the invention of new treatments. So why do we want to eliminate this position of evaluation from the start?

In my opinion, it is only the sick person who has a right to take this position. From his point of view, the question may seem justified as to what value his life as a sick person might have for science; after all, it is well known that many people leave their bodies to an anatomical institute in order to be able to serve science even after their lives have ended. From our point of view, however, from the doctor's point of view, this highly objective evaluation of human beings is unacceptable. Certainly, objectivity suits the doctor; the medical professional's attitude to the patient is necessarily one of inner distance. Just think of how a doctor's rounds at a hospital are made. With each patient, the doctor does not have the human being but the "case" in front of him. The assistant who "leads" the senior physician during his rounds introduces the patient to him as "a case of" this or that disease. In general, the doctor also tends to treat the disease and not the person, not the sick person. And repeatedly one hears the expression "that is a case of." Please note, "that," and not "this person here"; and further, "is," in other words, not "has," so there is no recognition of an illness that this human being has but only a case that this person "is"; lastly "a" case, meaning some arbitrary case, the mere representative of a particular disease—or perhaps case number so and so of a series, known as the disease "subject." With these expressions that creep unconsciously into medical jargon, it is sufficiently evident how deep and how far the tendency for dissociation by doctors extends, and their objectification of human beings.

A good doctor, who we all know to be a good person, will therefore always call himself back from objectivity to humanity. The more objective his attitude threatens to become (and it will become so, especially with regard to cases of mental illness), the more he will force himself to switch back to the human attitude, if only by occasionally asking himself: "Right, this is a case of schizophrenia. Now, what would I do in his place?" It is quite a different story that we do not want to explore further here, that this change back to the human, this turning away from the purely factual, scientific position to the human and, in fact, medical position, shows that it is the humanness in the doctor that first discovers the human in the patient (which is above all significant for the psychiatrist)—and, moreover, awakens the human in the patient (which, in turn, is mainly important in the field of psychiatric care).

So, if the question of the mere usefulness to human society and scientific progress of even the life of a sick person is raised, then this question already reveals an inhuman and therefore unmedical point of view, a position of radical objectification and degradation of human beings, which we reject from the outset. Even the mentally ill person "is" not just a disease to us but is first and foremost a human being, that is, a person who "has" an illness. And how human this person can be, even while being so unwell; how human she can be, not only despite and in her illness, but in her attitude to the illness. Many years ago, I got to know an old woman who had suffered from a severe mental disorder for decades and was per-petually tormented by hallucinations; she constantly heard voices that criticized everything she did with mocking remarks—certainly a most distressing state of affairs. But how this woman reacted to her terrible fate! How she reconciled herself to her fate! Because clearly that is what she had done: while she described her con-dition, her conversation was calm and cheerful; she had even remained industrious, as far as this was possible. Astonished by this, I allowed myself the cautious ques-tion of what she thought of this condition and how she could smile like that, and whether this continual hear-ing of voices was not too dreadful? And what was her re-ply? "My God, I just think, Doctor, it's still better that I hear voices than if I was deaf as a post." And she con-tinued to smile mischievously. What humanity, what hu-man achievement—one is compelled to say, what artful wisdom this statement contains!

On the other hand, let us ask ourselves what we have to say about the fact that incurably ill people, especially incurably mentally ill people, have been declared to be unworthy of life solely on the basis of their illness and have been threatened with destruction and even killed. Because we hear repeatedly that the killing of incurably mentally ill people would be the only justifiable measure that people "could still understand" within an otherwise unacceptable program of political ideology, that is why we would now like to examine all those reasons that, for the most part, are only the tacit basis for such remarks, and to elucidate them with counterarguments that are as watertight as possible.

Since, primarily, we are talking about whether we have the right to kill incurably mentally ill people whose lives are deemed meaningless and "unworthy of living," we must first ask, "What is meant by incurable?" Instead of giving you, as nonexperts, a number of not fully comprehensible and, above all, unverifiable explanations, I would like to confine myself to presenting a specific individual case that I myself witnessed. There was a young man in the hospital who was in a state of "complete inhibition": for five whole years he did not say a word and did not eat unaided, so that he had to be fed artificially with a tube through the nose; he stayed in bed day in, day out, so the muscles in his legs eventually wasted away. If I had pointed out this case on the occasion of one of the frequent doctors' tours around the hospital, one of the students would certainly have asked me, as so often: "Now tell me seriously, Doctor, would it not be better to let such a person die?" Well, the future would have given him the answer. For one day, for no apparent reason, our patient sat up, asked the nurse if he could eat his meal in the normal way, and also demanded to be helped out of bed in order to begin walking exercises. He behaved completely normally in other ways too, considering his situation. Gradually, his leg muscles began to get stronger, and it only took a few weeks for the patient to be "discharged as cured." Shortly after that, he not only returned to his former profession but also gave lectures at one of the adult education colleges in Vienna about trips abroad and alpine tours that he had made and of which he had brought back wonderful photos. However, once he also addressed a small, intimate group of my psychiatrist colleagues after I invited him to give a lecture on his inner life during those critical five years of his time in the institution. In this lecture, he described all kinds of interesting experiences from that time and gave us an insight into not only the spiritual wealth that had been hidden beneath the outer lack of movement but also many remarkable details of what was happening "behind the scenes," the happenings that a not particularly conscientious doctor who only makes his rounds and does not take notice of much otherwise has no idea of. The patient still remembered this or that event years later, much to the chagrin of some of the nurses, who probably never expected that the patient would recover and divulge his memories.

But even supposing that a certain case really is, by general consensus, incurable, who can say how long this case—namely, the illness in question—will truly remain incurable? Have we not seen in psychiatry, especially in the last few decades, that mental disorders that were hitherto classified as incurable could at least be alleviated if not completely cured by some kind of treatment? So who can say whether the particular case of the disorder we are now dealing with would be influenced by such a treatment, by a therapy that is currently being worked on somewhere in the world, in some hospital, without us having any idea of it?

We must now ask ourselves: Supposing we were as omniscient as we would need to be in order to speak with absolute certainty of not just temporary but permanent incurability; who would then give the doctor the right to kill? Is the doctor ever employed by society to kill? Doesn't he rather have the task to save where he can and to give care whenever he is unable to heal? (It is no coincidence that most psychiatric hospitals are expressly called *Heil- und Pflegeanstalten* [healing and care institutions].) The doctor as such is certainly not a judge over the "being and nonbeing" of the sick people entrusted to him, or who even entrust themselves to him. Therefore, from the outset, he has no right—and should never presume so—to pass judgment on the apparent value or worthlessness of the lives of allegedly or actually incurable patients.

Just imagine what would happen if this "right" (which he does not, in fact, have) were raised to the level of a law (even if it were only unwritten). I'll tell you: the trust of patients and their relatives in the medical profession would be destroyed forever! Because no one would ever know whether the doctor was still approaching them as helper and healer or already as judge and executioner.

Now you may raise further objections: perhaps you will take the position that the counterarguments I have presented are not watertight, since we honestly have to ask ourselves whether the state has a duty to grant the doctor the right to destroy superfluous, useless individuals. After all, it would be conceivable that the state, as the guardian of public interest, should free the community of the burden of these highly "unproductive" individuals who consume the bread of the people who are healthy and fit for life.

Well, when it comes to the consumption of goods such as food, hospital beds, the work of doctors and nurses, the consideration of these resources is irrelevant to a discussion about this argument if we keep one thing in mind: a state that is already economically so badly off that it relies on eliminating the relatively insignificant percentage of its incurable citizens in order to save on those aforementioned goods—such a state has already reached the end economically.

When examining the other side of the question, the fact that incurable patients are no longer useful to society, that caring for them therefore represents "unproductive" care, it should be remembered that usefulness to society is not and can never be the only criterion that we are justified in applying to a person. It is not difficult to find proof on this subject: the patients with dementia in psychiatric institutions, who carry out their simple work there, pushing a wheelbarrow full of tiles or even just helping to wash the dishes, these people are much more useful and productive than our grandparents, who spend their twilight years highly unproductively and whose elimination for the sole reason that they are unproductive would be opposed by the very same people who would otherwise advocate the destruction of unproductive life. Just think how unproductive the existence of an old woman is, sitting there at home, dozing and half paralyzed in the armchair by the window, and yet, how she is surrounded and cosseted by the love of her children and grandchildren! Surrounded by this love, she is this particular grandmother—no more and no less. But as such, within this love, she is as indispensable and irreplaceable as another person who is still working in his job and is indispensable and irreplaceable regarding his service to the community! In the first part, when we talked about the fact that the uniqueness and individuality of every human being constitutes the value of his person, and that this value must be related to a community to which this uniqueness is of value, then we were all thinking of it primarily in terms of serving the community; but now we can see that there is also a second way in which the person as a unique and individual being always comes into his own, in which the value of his personality is also realized and his personal, specific meaning of life is fulfilled: this is the way of love, or better still, of being loved. This is more or less a passive path, without any striving, without any doing—"without doing anything for it"—in being loved, what someone otherwise had to strive for in his activity or employment now seems to fall into his lap; on this path of being loved he achieves the things he would normally have to fight for and win through his performance, but without needing to earn them: indeed one cannot earn love; love is not a reward, but a blessing. On the path of love a person thus receives by "grace" the things he would otherwise have to strive for or obtain through action: the realization of both his uniqueness and his individuality. For it is the nature of love that makes us see our loved one in their uniqueness and individuality.

Now, I am prepared for the following argument: everything I have said probably applies in general but is perhaps hardly true of those poor beings who somehow wrongly hold the title of "human"—perhaps for severely mentally disabled children. But you will be astonished (the experienced psychiatrist is by no means surprised) if I explain to you that one sees again and again how these very children are particularly cherished and cosseted with the tenderest love on the part of their parents. Just allow me to read you a passage from the letter of a mother who lost her child in the course of the notorious euthanasia program:

> Due to an early malformation of the skull bones in the womb, my child was born on 6 June 1929 as incurably ill. I myself was 18 years old. I adored my child and loved her beyond measure. My mother and I did everything we could to help the poor little mite, but in vain. The child could not walk or speak, but I was young and did not give up hope. I worked day and night just to buy my beloved girl nutritional supplements and medication. And when I put her small, thin hands around my neck and said to her, "Do you love

me, my girl?" she hugged me very tightly, laughed, and clumsily stroked my face with her little hands. Then I was happy, in spite of everything, infinitely happy.

But I see that you still have some arguments, at least apparently. Because in the end you could assert that, in the above-mentioned cases of mental illness, the doctor who kills an incurable patient is acting ultimately as a representative of the well-understood will of the patients concerned, as it were. Simply because this will is "deranged," precisely because these patients are not aware of their own will and their own true interests due to their mental disorder—for that reason the doctor must be a kind of attorney for their will, not only justified but almost obliged to carry out the killing.

One could consider, if understood correctly, that such a killing would be a substitute for a suicide, which the patient would undoubtedly undertake if only he knew the truth of his situation.

What I would like to say to you in answer to this argument, I will explain by means of another case I experienced: As a young doctor I was working in a clinic for internal medicine to which one day a young colleague was admitted. He had already brought the diagnosis with him—a diagnosis of a highly dangerous, no longer operable, and particularly unusual and malignant type of cancer—and his diagnosis was correct! This was a special form of cancer—medically described as melanosarcoma—which is detectable through a specific urinary reaction. Of course, we tried to deceive the patient: we exchanged his urine with that of another patient and showed him the negative result of the reaction. But what did he do? One night, at midnight, he crept into the lab and set up the test for his own urine to surprise us with his positive result the next day during the doctors' rounds. We were extremely embarrassed, and there was nothing left but to expect our colleague to commit suicide. Every time he had permission to leave the hospital—and we could hardly have forbidden him to go—to visit his usual little cafe nearby, we were on tenterhooks in case we heard that he had poisoned himself in the cafe toilet. But what really happened? The more visibly the disease progressed, the more the patient began to doubt his diagnosis; even when he had metastases in his liver, he began to postulate harmless liver diseases. So, what had occurred? The nearer the end of his life came, the more this man's will to live asserted itself and the less he wanted to admit to his approaching end. Whichever way you look at it, the fact is and remains that his will to live was raging, and this fact must remind us unequivocally and once and for all (and is applicable to all similar cases) that we do not have the right to deny any patient this will to live!

I would go so far as to defend this thesis even where we as doctors are confronted with a fait accompli where a person has proved through his or her actions that they no longer have the will to live. I mean the suicides. And I take the position that even in the case of an actual suicide attempt, the doctor not only has the right but also the duty to intervene medically, and that means to save and to help if, and to the extent that, he can. At one time this question would not have been without relevance. Years ago, I was myself engaged in developing a procedure that would save patients in even the most severe cases of poisoning with sleeping pills, in which every hitherto usual treatment had failed. There were voices raised in protest from colleagues who wanted to point out that, for people whose decision to commit suicide was understandable from a human point of view (there was a whole suicide epidemic in the face of extremely threatening circumstances that endangered a particular group of people),[9] I did not have the right to "return life to them" or to drag them back into life. What I was doing—that was the argument—was playing the role of fate. However, I insisted on my own point of view. And I did not even give up this principle when my own assistant, who had also repeatedly criticized this approach, was one day admitted to the hospital after a suicide attempt: in her case too, I held firmly to my principle, and in her case too, I applied my technique—not receiving any thanks, to be sure, but successfully. But what I explained to the critics of my method on moral grounds (naturally, medical criticism would have been refuted by the facts) was something like this: It is not I who wishes to play the role of destiny but the doctor who abandons a suicide to his fate, who gives fate free reign and sits on his hands where he could perhaps still intervene to help, is the one who tries to act the part of destiny. Because if it had pleased "fate" to really allow the suicide in question to perish, then this fate would certainly have found ways and means to prevent the dying person from falling into the hands of a doctor while there was still time. However, once the patient has been delivered into the hands of the doctor, then this doctor must act like a doctor and not fall into the arms of *this particular* fate, i.e., a "merciful" fate.

Now, I hope I have shown you, through this discussion of all the apparent arguments that could support euthanasia, how unconditional is the meaningfulness of existence and therefore how unshakeable is our belief in meaning in our lives. If, at first, life as such proved to be meaningful to us, it later emerged that even suffering contributes to meaning and is part of the meaning of life. And then we saw that even dying can have meaning, that it can be meaningful "to die one's own death." And finally, it was seen that even illness, even incurable illness, yes, even incurable mental illness, does not give anyone the right to judge a human life as being "unworthy of life" and deny them the right to life. Thus, we appear to have explored the question of the meaning of life a little, from various angles. In a rough review of our main conclusion, we remember above all our basic observation that life itself means being questioned and that we cannot justifiably ask about its meaning, since this meaning exists in the act of answering. But we said that the answers that we must give to life's specific questions can no longer exist in words but only in deeds, and more than that in living, in our whole being! The questions of "our lives" can, as we felt, only be answered by each of us being responsible for "our own lives."

In conclusion, we must not forget that the original question about meaning can also be given a different expression, that it can also be meant differently, insofar as it can be asked in relation to the whole world, especially regarding what happens to us, what we encounter, involuntarily and unavoidably, in relation to fate. We are not able to direct fate—we describe fate as whatever we have no influence over, whatever escapes the power of our will. Certainly, we have seen that the meaning of our lives consists in no small part in how we relate to our external fate, how we behave toward it when we can no longer shape it or when it is unalterable from the outset. But, going a step further, we must now ask whether it is conceivable that even this pure, true fate, and with it, beyond it, everything that is happening out there in the universe, has any meaning?

I believe that here we are presented with two major options for our way of thinking, each of which is irrefutable, and unprovable! After all, we could well assert that everything is, in the end, completely meaningless, just as we could state that everything is not only highly meaningful but so meaningful that we can no longer comprehend the meaning of the whole, this universal meaning; that we could, in fact, only speak of an "ultimate meaning of the world." Therefore, one could argue for the total meaninglessness of the world with the same justification as one could argue for an ultimate meaning of the world. With the same justification, which means in this case with the same justified or unjustified logic. In fact, the decision we are faced with is no longer a logical decision. It would be as logical to argue for the one as for the other. In logic, both options for our way of thinking are real thinking options. The decision we are talking about here is, logically speaking, an unfounded decision; it has nothing as a foundation, its foundation is nothing: in this decision we hover above the abyss of nothingness— but at the same time in this decision we are standing at the horizon of ultimate meaning! A person cannot take this decision on the basis of a logical rule but only from the depths of his or her own being, that is the only way to decide in favor of one or the other. But we do know one thing: if a human being decides to believe in an ultimate meaning, in the super-meaning of being, then this belief, like every belief, will have a creative effect. Because belief is not just belief in one's "own" truth, it is more, much more: belief brings into being that which is believed! Therefore, we can say that to decide on *one particular* option for our way of thinking is more than the *mere choice* of a possibility of thinking—it is the *bringing into being* of this mere *option of thought.*

EXPERIMENTUM
CRUCIS

THERE IS A SMALL TOWN IN BAVARIA CALLED LANDSBERG, about fifty kilometers west of Munich. South of it, a road leads to the town of Markt Kaufering, five kilometers away. At the beginning of last year as day was dawning, 280 men marched along this street. The column consisted of rows of five and was escorted by SS soldiers: this was a group of prisoners from the concentration camp in Kaufering. They walked to a nearby forest, where they were to build a concealed munitions factory of enormous proportions. These were ragged, down-and-out figures walking along this street. Walking is the wrong description; they hobbled, they dragged themselves along, in many cases hanging on to each other and supporting one another; their legs, swollen and bulging from hunger edema, could barely support their bodies, weighing, on average, only forty kilograms. Their feet ached, for they were raw, covered in festering pressure sores and ulcerated chilblains. And what was going on in the brains of these men? They thought about the soup that was doled out for their only meal of the day in the evening at the camp, after returning from the work site, and wondered whether, that evening, as well as the watery broth, they would be lucky enough to grab a potato floating in it. And they thought about which group they would be assigned to in the next quarter of an hour when work started: whether they would end up in one of the groups under a dreaded foreman or one of the relatively pleasant ones. And, so, the thoughts of these people revolved around the daily troubles of a concentration camp inmate.

Then one of the men felt that these thoughts were somehow too pointless. And he tried rise above them and think other thoughts, more decent, human concerns. But he was not quite able to do it. Then he used a trick: he tried to distance himself from this whole agonizing life, to get beyond it by looking at it, as they say, from a higher vantage point or from the viewpoint of the future, in the sense of a future theoretical observation. And what did he do? He imagined that he was standing before a lectern at a Viennese adult education college and giving a lecture, and it would be about what he was currently experiencing: in his mind, he gave a lecture entitled "Psychology of the Concentration Camp."

If you had looked more closely at that man in that group, you would have noticed that he had sewn onto his coat and his trousers small scraps of linen on which a number was visible: 119104. And if you had looked through the Dachau camp records, you would have found that beside this number was written the name of the camp inmate: Frankl Viktor.

Now, for the first time, I would like to really give that lecture in this real hall of this Vienna adult education college, the lecture that this man had given in his mind at that time. Let me tell you about it! That lecture began with the words: In the psychology of the concentration camp we can discern several phases in terms of the psychological reactions of the camp prisoners to life in the camp. The first phase is at the time of the prisoners' admission to the camp. This is the phase that could be identified and characterized as admission shock. Imagine: the prisoner is delivered off to, let's say, Auschwitz. If he belonged, as was the case with my transport, to the majority of around 95 percent, then his path would lead from the train station directly to one of the gas chambers; but if he belonged, as by chance I did, to the minority of 5 percent, then his path led first to the disinfection chamber, so into a real . . . shower. Before he can enter the actual shower room, everything that he has with him is taken away, he is only allowed to keep his braces or belt, at best his spectacles or a truss. But no hair is allowed to remain on his body, he is completely shaven. When he is finally standing under the shower, nothing has remained of his whole former life except his literally "naked" existence. And now he reaches the actual point at which he enters the first phase of the experience of the concentration camp: he puts a line through his entire former existence.

No one will be surprised to hear that his next thought concerns the question of how best to commit suicide.

In fact, everyone in this situation flirts, if only for a moment, with the idea of "running into the wire," committing suicide, using the usual method in the camp: contact with the high voltage barbed-wire fence. However, he drops his intention at once, simply because it has become more or less pointless; because a suicide attempt is redundant in this situation inasmuch as the average probability of not, sooner or later, going to the gas chamber is in any case minimal. Who needs to run into the wire when he is going into the gas sooner or later? He no longer needs to wish for the "wire" once he has the "gas" to be afraid of, but he no longer needs to fear the "gas" once he has wished for the "wire."

When I talk of these things, I always tell of the following experience: On the first morning that we spent in Auschwitz, a colleague of mine, who had arrived a few weeks before us, smuggled himself into our quarters—as newcomers we were all together in a separate hut. He wanted to comfort us and warn us. Above all, he made us understand that we should pay great attention to our appearance; we should strive, at all costs, to give the impression of being fit for work. Even a limp, perhaps for a reason that is trivial in itself—for example, because of ill-fitting shoes—would be enough; an SS man who saw somebody limping would be capable of simply waving them aside and sending them straight to the gas chamber. Only people who were fit for work would be considered fit to live; all the rest would be judged to be unworthy of life, unworthy of survival!

This is why my colleague urged us to shave every day so that, after scraping the skin on our faces with some kind of improvised shaving implement, such as a piece of broken glass, we would look "rosier," fresher, healthier. And when he finally inspected our group to see if we all made the right impression of good health and fitness for work, he said reassuringly: "As you stand before me now, you don't need to be afraid of being sent to the gas chamber for the time being—maybe except one—except you, Frankl. You are not angry with me, are you? But you are the only one who, going on appearance, might currently be considered for selection." (*Selection* was the commonly used term in the camp for choosing those who would be sent to the gas chamber with the next batch.) Well, I was not angry with him in the least, because what I felt at that moment was the satisfaction that at least this way I would almost certainly be spared a suicide attempt.

This indifference to one's own fate then continues further. Increasingly, even within a few days of his imprisonment in the camp, the inmate becomes more and more emotionally numbed. Things that are going on around him affect him less and less. Whereas in the first few days, the sheer abundance of experiences filled with ugliness—hateful in every sense—provoke feelings of horror, outrage, and disgust, these feelings eventually subside, and inner life as a whole is reduced to a minimum; something that for an outsider would be entirely unimaginable. All thought and striving are then restricted to surviving only for today. All spiritual life is likewise reduced to serve this sole interest. In relation to everything else, the soul surrounds itself with a protective shell from which the otherwise harrowing and disturbing impressions will bounce off. This is how the soul protects itself, how it tries to safeguard itself from the overwhelming power threatening to swamp it and tries to preserve its equilibrium—to rescue itself into indifference. In this way, the prisoner progresses into the second phase of his psychological reaction to camp life: the phase that could be characterized as the phase of apathy.

But if your exclusive interest is now self-preservation, preserving the lives of yourself and a few friends, then the inner life of the individual sinks almost to the level of an animal. And if we look more closely we might add, to the level of a herd animal. To verify this, one would have had to observe the behavior of the camp inmates when they formed a marching column, whereby they were mainly concerned with positioning themselves in the middle of the procession and in the middle of a row of five, so that they were not so exposed to the kicks of the guards. Each man's efforts were primarily directed at not attracting attention, not standing out in any way, but just disappearing into the mass. No wonder, then, if this submerging into the mass led to a "going under," a decline of the personal sphere. In the camp the human being threatened to become a creature of the masses. On average he became as primitive as a mass creature. His whole driving force became primitive. It became primitive insofar as it was an attitude of compulsion. So, it is easy to understand that psychoanalysts among my colleagues who were with me in the concentration camp spoke in their own terms of a "regression": regression means the retreat of the psyche to more primitive stages of animal impulse. In fact, it was possible, by observing the typical dreams of the prisoners, to determine to what primitive wishes they were inwardly giving themselves. So, what did the men mainly dream of in the camp? Always the same: bread, cigarettes, decent ground coffee, and, last but not least, a nice warm bath (and I personally always dreamt of a very particular gateau).

And yet the opinion of my one-sided, psychoanalytically orientated colleagues was fundamentally wrong. It is not true that the experience of the concentration camp drove people to regression out of a fateful necessity and forced them internally to take a step backward. I know of many cases—and even though they are individual ones, they still have fundamental evidential value—in which the people concerned, far from inwardly regressing, instead made inner progress, growing beyond themselves and achieving true human greatness, even in the concentration camp and precisely through their experience of the concentration camp.

Now, other professionals, non-psychoanalysts, have a different interpretation of what happened to people's mental and spiritual life in the concentration camp. The well-known characterologist Professor [Emil] Utitz, who himself spent several years in a concentration camp, thought he could observe that the character of camp inmates generally developed according to the psychological type that Kretschmer calls the schizoid.[10] This type is characterized by the fact that the afflicted person swings between the affective states of apathy on the one hand and irritability on the other, while the most important other type, characterized by the cycloid temperament,[11] is "rejoicing to high heaven" one minute and "in the depths of despair"[12] the next; in other words, he is caught in a permanent cycle of joyful excitement and depressive sadness. This is not the place to go into a specialist discussion of this psychopathological outlook. I would like to limit myself to what is fundamentally important, and that is the conclusion I was able to draw from the identical observation "material," contrary to Utitz: namely, that the person in the concentration camp is by no means under any external compulsion to get involved in directing his inner development toward becoming the "typical KZler" [concentration camp prisoner] with those (apparent) schizoid tendencies, but that instead he retains a freedom, the human freedom to adapt to his fate, his environment, in one way or another—and indeed there was a "one way or another"! And there were people in the camp, who, for example, were able to overcome their apathy and suppress their irritability, and in the end it was a question of appealing to their ability to "do things differently" and not just the supposed compulsion to "do things this way"! That inner ability, that real human freedom—they could not take that away from the prisoner, even if, in there, they could take everything else away from him and, in fact, did so. This freedom stayed with him, even when the spectacles that they let him keep were smashed to pieces by a punch to the face, and even when one day he was forced to exchange his belt for a piece of bread, so that finally nothing remained of his last few belongings—but that freedom was left in him and it remained with him until his last breath!

Even if a man lapsed into the psychological conformity of the concentration camp, he nevertheless had the freedom to escape the power and influence of that environment and not to be governed by those rules but to resist them, to withdraw from them instead of obeying them blindly. In other words, that man did once possess such freedom; but he had given it away, he had, as it were, renounced its use—voluntarily renounced it! But in so doing he had given himself up, abandoned his self, his very essence. Spiritually, he had let himself fall.

But now we need to ask, when did this deterioration back to type begin, when did this person allow himself to fall spiritually? And our answer must be, Once he had lost his inner hold—as soon as he no longer had an inner hold! Such hold could exist in two forms: either it was a hold on the future or a hold on eternity. The latter was the case with all truly religious people; they did not even need a hold on the future, their future life out there in the free world, after their coming liberation—these people could remain upright irrespective of whether they anticipated a future destiny, or would even experience such a future, or survive the concentration camp. The others, however, were forced to find a hold on their future life, on the content of their life in the future. But it was hard for them to think about the future, their thinking about it could find no reference point, no end point: an end—the end—could not be foreseen. How enviable it seemed to us to be a serious criminal who knew exactly that he had to serve his term of ten years, who could calculate how many days had to pass until the date of his release . . . lucky man! Because all of us in the camp did not have and did not know of a "release date," and none of us knew when the end would come. This was, according to the unanimous opinion of my comrades, perhaps one of the most spiritually depressing facts of life in the camp! And the recurrent rumors of an imminent end to the war only increased the torment of waiting. For again and again the deadlines had to be postponed. But who could have gone on believing such news? During a full three years I heard repeatedly: in six weeks the war will be over, we will be home again in six weeks at most. The disappointment became ever more bitter and more profound, the expectation more fearful. And what does the Bible say? "Hope deferred makes the heart sick."[13] Indeed, it gets sick, so sick that it eventually stops beating. You will understand this when I tell you about the following case: At the beginning of March last year, my former block elder, a Budapest tango composer and librettist for light operas, told me that he had had a strange dream. "Around the middle of February I dreamt," he said, "that a voice spoke to me and told me I should make a wish, I should ask the voice something I wanted to know; it could answer the question, it could predict my future. And then I asked the voice: 'When will the war be over for me, do you understand? For me: so when will we be liberated by the advancing American troops?'" "And what answer did the voice give you?" Then he leaned toward me and whispered secretively in my ear: "On the 30th of March!" In mid-March I was admitted to the infirmary hut with typhus. On April 1st I was released from there and returned to my earthen hut: "Where is the block elder?" I asked, and what did I discover? Toward the end of March, when the date predicted by the voice in his dream had moved ever closer without the military situation seeming to keep up with it, our block elder had become increasingly depressed. On the 29th of March he started running a high temperature. On the 30th of March, the day the war was to end "for him," he lost consciousness. On the 31st of March he was dead. He had died of typhus.

So you can see that spiritual and mental decline due to losing one's inner hold, especially due to the loss of a hold on the future, also leads to physical decline. Now let us ask ourselves whether there was any therapy for this mental, spiritual, and physical decline: whether one could have done anything about it—and what? I can only give you this answer: there was a therapy, but it is clear that, from the outset, it had to be confined to the psychological so that it could only be a psychotherapy. And within such psychotherapy, of course, it was primarily a matter of providing a spiritual hold, of giving life content. Thinking of the words of Nietzsche who once said, "Whoever has a why to live can bear almost any how"—a "why," that is part of the content of life, and the "how," those were the conditions of life that made camp life so difficult that it only became bearable with regard to a "why," a wherefore. So if there was basically nothing other than psychotherapy to enable people to endure the camp, then this psychotherapy was already defined in a particular sense, since it needed to endeavor to convince the person who was being asked to muster the will to survive that this survival had meaning. In addition, the psychotherapeutic task, which in the camp was truly the task of caring for the inmates' souls, was made more difficult because we were dealing with people who, in general, on average, could not count on surviving! What could you have said to them? And one should have said something to them in particular. And hence this situation became the *experimentum crucis* for that psychotherapeutic care.[14]

I have already said in the previous part that not only life itself but also the suffering involved has a meaning, and in fact a meaning that is so unconditional that it can be fulfilled even where the suffering does not lead to outward success, where it looks as though the suffering was in vain. And it was mainly such suffering that we had to deal with in the concentration camps. But what ought I have said to these people who were lying next to me in the barracks and knew pretty accurately that they would die and how soon they would die? They knew as well as I did that no life, no person, and no task (remember the double case that I told you about in the first part[15]) would be waiting for them, or that it would be waiting in vain. . . . So, as well as the meaning of living, of survival, it was also important to point out the meaning of suffering and of suffering in vain—indeed, much more than this—even to reveal the meaning that may be latent in death! A death, of course, that could have been more meaningful only in the sense of Rilke's maxim of which we spoke last time, and which said that each person should die his or her own death. It was essential that we should die a death of our own and not the death that the SS had forced on us! We bear responsibility for this task just as we bear responsibility for the task of life. Responsibility? To whom, to which higher authority? And who would be allowed to answer this question for anyone else? Does not everyone have to decide this ultimate question for himself? What does it matter if maybe one man in the barracks felt responsible to his conscience and another to his God and a third to a person who was now far away? Each one of them knew that somehow, somewhere, someone was there, unseen, watching over him, who demanded of him that he would be "worthy of his sufferings," as Dostoevsky once said, and expected of him that he should "die his own death." Each of us felt this expectation at that time when death was near, and we felt it all the more the less we felt that we ourselves could still expect anything from life, that someone or something was still waiting for us at all, and that we might expect to survive at all.

Many of you who have not lived through the concentration camp will be astonished and will ask me how a human being can endure all the things I have been talking about. I assure you, the person who has experienced and survived all of that is even more amazed than you are! But do not forget this: the human psyche seems to behave in some ways like a vaulted arch—an arch that has become dilapidated can be supported by placing an extra load on it. The human soul also appears to be strengthened by experiencing a burden (at least to a particular degree and within certain limits). This is how, and this is the only way we can understand it, many a weakling was able to leave the concentration camp in a better, stronger state of mind, as it were, than when he had entered it. At the same time, however, we now understand that the liberation, the release from the camp, the sudden release of the prisoner from the intense pressure he has been under all that time, in turn endangers his psyche. I use caisson disease, or decompression sickness, for comparison in this context. It affects divers who work underwater under high atmospheric pressure and should never suddenly be returned to normal air pressure, but only gradually, because otherwise they suffer the most serious physical consequences.

However, this also anticipates our discussion of the third and final phase within the psychology of the concentration camp, the psychology of the liberated inmate. The most important thing I want to say regarding him concerns something that will, no doubt, greatly astonish you: it is the fact that it takes many days before the liberated person is able to enjoy his liberation. He must actually and literally relearn how to be happy. And sometimes he has to hurry to learn this, because often he will soon need to unlearn it again and must learn to suffer again. I would like to say a little about that now.

Imagine that the man liberated from the concentration camp returns, comes home. Then he may be met with some kind of a shrug of the shoulders. And above all, he will always hear two phrases from other people: "We did not know anything about it," and "We also suffered." Let us start with the second statement and ask ourselves first whether human suffering can be measured or assessed in such a way that the suffering of one person can be compared to the suffering of another. And I would like to say about this that the suffering of human beings is incommensurable! Real suffering fills a person completely, fills their whole being.

I once talked to a friend about my experiences in the concentration camp; he himself had not been in a camp, he had "merely" fought at Stalingrad. And the man felt, as he said, somehow ashamed when compared with me. He did not need to be. There is indeed an essential difference between what a man experiences in battle and what he experiences in a concentration camp. In battle, he faces nothingness, he stares death in the face, but in the camp we ourselves were nothing, we were already dead during our lifetime. We were worth nothing. We did not only see nothingness, that is what we were. Our life counted for nothing; our death counted for nothing. There was no halo, not even a notional one, around our death. It was the departure of a small nothing into the vast nothingness. And this death was also barely noticed. We had already "lived" it long in advance!

And what would have happened if I had died in the camp? On the parade ground the next morning, someone in one of the rows of five, outwardly unmoved—standing there as usual with his face buried in his open coat collar against the frost, and his shoulders hunched— would have mumbled to the man next to him: "Frankl died yesterday," and at most this man would have murmured, "Hmm."

And in spite of everything, no human suffering can be compared to anyone else's because it is part of the nature of suffering that it is the suffering of a particular person, that it is *his or her own* suffering—that its "magnitude" is dependent solely on the sufferer, that is, on the person; a person's solitary suffering is just as unique and individual as is every person.

Therefore, it would be pointless to speak of differences in the magnitude of suffering; but a difference that truly matters is that between meaningful and meaningless suffering. But—and I think you will have gathered this sufficiently from previous lectures—this difference depends entirely on the individual human being: the individual, and only that individual, determines whether their suffering is meaningful or not. And what about the suffering of those people who, as we have heard, so strongly declare that they "also suffered," and they "had known of nothing"? You see, it is precisely this claim to having known nothing that, in my opinion, is so well suited to making meaningless the fact of having suffered. And why? Because it comes from an ethical misunderstanding of the situation. A misunderstanding that we will now address, not because I want to bring the politics of the day into the debate, but because I think it is necessary to augment the "metaphysics of everyday life" that we have concerned ourselves with so far, by adding an "ethics of everyday life."

We spoke earlier about the "why" of not-knowing, and said it was a misunderstanding; but if we ask about the cause of this misunderstanding, then we may discover that this "not-knowing" is in fact a "not wanting to know." What lies behind it is wanting to escape responsibility. However, the average person today is in fact being driven to flee responsibility. What is driving him to this flight is the fear of having to accept collective guilt. He will be declared guilty on all counts, complicit in things he has not done himself, indeed, things of which, in many cases, he actually "knew nothing." Should the decent person really be held accountable for the offenses of others, even if the offenders belong to the same nation? Was he, this decent man, not himself the victim of an offense, the object of a terror that was carried out by a ruling, leading class of his own people without him being able to stand up against the terror? Did he not suffer under it himself? Would not the establishment of a collective guilt be a relapse into exactly that worldview that we want to combat? That worldview that declares an individual guilty because others from the same group to which he happens to belong have actually or allegedly committed some kind of offense? And how ridiculous this outlook seems to us today—finally! Holding someone to account because of their nationality, native language, or place of birth must seem as ridiculous to us today as making them responsible for their own height. If a criminal who is 1.64 meters tall is arrested, should I also be hanged because I happen to be the same height?

But here we have to make an important distinction: we have to differentiate between collective guilt and collective liability. If I illustrate this with an allegorical example, you will understand me immediately. If I suddenly get appendicitis, is it my fault? Certainly not; and yet, if I have to have an operation, what then? I will nevertheless owe the fee for the operation to the doctor who operated on me. That is, I am "liable" for the settlement of the doctor's bill. So "liability without guilt" definitely exists. And it is a similar situation now with the collective of people who were collectively freed from terror. They could not liberate themselves; other collectives, other freedom-loving nations had to step in, join the battle, and sacrifice their best people, their youth, to liberate a nation that was powerless against its own leadership, from those leaders. This powerlessness had nothing to do with guilt. But would it be unfair, unjust, to have to pay for this liberation with some kind of sacrifice and to feel jointly liable, even if you were not complicit and knew you were not guilty?

If you want to understand the last chapter of this psychology, you would have had to accompany me at sunset on that spring evening last year, after the liberation of the Turkheim concentration camp, when I went alone into the woodland near the camp. There, on the highly illegal order of our camp commander, the comrades who had died in the camp were buried (the commander was the SS man who I mentioned in the first part who had paid for medicines for "his" camp prisoners out of his own pocket). During the burial, contrary to the orders this man had received, he did not neglect to ensure that, after removing slivers of bark from the slender trunks of the young fir trees that stood behind the mass graves, the names of the dead were inconspicuously scrawled there in indelible pencil. If you had been with me then, you would have sworn with me to ensure that the continuing life of us survivors would absolve the guilt of all of us— yes, *the guilt of all of us*! Because we survivors knew very well that the best among us in the camp did not come out, it was *the best* who did not return! So we could not perceive our survival as anything other than undeserved mercy. To earn it later, to earn it retrospectively and be halfway worthy of it, that, we felt, we owed our dead comrades. It only seemed possible to settle this guilt by shaking up and keeping alert the consciences of others as well as our own.

True enough, what became of the liberated man after such an experience, when he returned home, only too often made him forget that oath. However, there are moments in his life—and those are the significant ones—in which he fulfills what he once swore to himself: to bless the smallest piece of bread, the fact that he can sleep in a bed, that he does not have to stand for roll call or live in constant danger of death. Everything becomes relative for him and so does every misfortune. As we said, he who was literally nothing feels literally born again, but not as the person he was but as the essence of himself. In the first part I pointed out how everything extraneous to his person was "melted down." Not much of his ambition will have been left either. What may have lasted can at most be a yearning to achieve a far higher form of yearning, the urge for *self-realization*—only in its most essential form.

As you no doubt realize, we have, at the same time, reached the end of this topic and the limits of our discussion. No talking, no lectures can help us get any further—there is only one thing left for us to do: to act; namely, to act in our everyday lives.

We were just talking about everyday life; yes, even the phrase "metaphysics of everyday life" came up. I hope that you now understand this expression correctly: it was not enough to make transparent the everyday—which is only apparently so gray, banal, and commonplace—so that we can look through it into the eternal; but in the final analysis it was necessary to point out that the eternal refers back to the temporal—to the temporal, the everyday, and the point of an ongoing encounter between the finite and the infinite. What we create, experience, and suffer, in this time, we create, experience, and suffer for all eternity. As far as we bear responsibility for an event, as far as it is "history," our responsibility, it is incredibly burdened by the fact that something that has happened cannot be "taken out of the world." However, at the same time, an appeal is made to our responsibility—precisely to bring what has not yet happened *into* the world! And each of us must do this as part of our daily work, as part of our everyday lives. So everyday life becomes the reality per se, and this reality becomes the potential for action. And so, the "metaphysics of everyday life" only at first leads us out of everyday life, but then—consciously and responsibly—it leads us back into everyday life.

What leads us forward and helps us along the way, what has guided and is guiding us, is a joy in taking responsibility. But to what extent is the average person happy to take on responsibility?

Responsibility is something one is both "drawn to" and "withdraws from." This wisdom in the language indicates that there are opposing forces in human beings that prevent them from taking responsibility. And indeed, there is something unfathomable about responsibility: the longer and the more deeply we look into it, the more we become aware of it, until finally we are seized by a kind of dizziness. If we delve into the nature of human responsibility, we recoil: there is something terrible about the responsibility of a human being—and at the same time something glorious!

It is terrible to know that at every moment I bear responsibility for the next; that every decision, from the smallest to the largest, is a decision "for all eternity"; that in every moment I can actualize the possibility of a moment, of that particular moment, or forfeit it. Every single moment contains thousands of possibilities—and I can only choose one of them to actualize it. But in making the choice, I have condemned all the others and sentenced them to "never being," and even this is for all eternity! But it is wonderful to know that the future—my own future and with it the future of the things, the people around me—is somehow, albeit to a very small extent, dependent on my decisions in every moment. Everything I realize through them, or "bring into the world," as we have said, I save into reality and thus protect from transience.

But on average, people are too sluggish to shoulder their responsibilities. And this is where education for responsibility begins. Certainly, the burden is heavy, it is difficult not only to recognize responsibility but also to commit to it. To say yes to it, and to life. But there have been people who have said yes despite all difficulties. And when the inmates in the Buchenwald concentration camp sang in their song, "We still want to say yes to life," they did not only sing about it but also achieved it many times—they and many of us in the other camps as well. And they achieved it under unspeakable conditions, external and internal conditions that we have already spoken enough about today. So shouldn't we all be able to achieve it today in, after all, incomparably milder circumstances? To say yes to life is not only meaningful under all circumstances—because life itself is—but it is also possible under all circumstances.

And ultimately that was the entire purpose of these three parts: to show you that people can still—despite hardship and death (first part), despite suffering from physical or mental illness (second part) or under the fate of the concentration camp (third part)—say yes to life in spite of everything.

AFTERWORD

In Vienna the war ended on April 13, 1945. Two weeks later, the day of liberation came for the concentration camp inmate Viktor Frankl. But it would still take until August before he could return to Vienna, where the most dreadful news awaited him. His despair and his struggle for the strength to go on living are evident in the harrowing letters he wrote to relatives and friends in the first weeks after his return home.[15]

Frankl plunged into his work, and rarely has the use of this phrase been more apposite. He took over the management of the neurological department of the Vienna Policlinic; in just a few months he wrote two books; at the adult education college in Ottakring, with which he had been closely connected since the 1930s, he held a series of lectures in autumn 1945 entitled "The Mentally Ill Person"; he commented on issues of the day regarding politics, society, and culture in numerous newspaper articles and in public discussions. In his journalistic fervor, he met an audience that was intellectually and culturally starved after the years of war and the mental narrowness of the Nazi regime. Thus, in a time when there was disorientation and a lack of guidance, he became a sought-after discussion partner in public forums, as well as in medical and philosophical circles. His topics were guilt and responsibility—surely a topic for the times!—covering fear of life, everyday ethics, and, repeatedly, the confrontation with the inhumane ideologies of the recent past. First and foremost, however, Frankl was always concerned with psychotherapy, both for the individual patient and at a collective level. The course directory of the adult education college at Ottakring for the 1946 summer semester contains the following entry:

> Dr. Viktor Frankl: Issues of our times and everyday problems viewed from the perspective of a psychiatrist. Five lectures (Suicide—Forced annihilation—The world of the mentally ill—Sexual education—Concentration camp). Saturdays 5–6 pm. Starting 23 March.

On the day the course started, Frankl published a newspaper article, "Vienna and Psychiatric Care." At the end of the article, he states:

> But in Vienna, the spirit of psychotherapy is still alive, and in spite of everything, and hopefully as soon as possible, we can expect that Vienna, the birthplace of psychiatric healing, will also be the site of its rebirth. The rebirth of a psychotherapy that is aware of its role

in society—especially in times of internal and external distress—and of its responsibility to a world that is waiting for both spiritual and material rebuilding.[16]

On the basis of the Ottakring lecture series Frankl wrote the book *Say Yes to Life in Spite of Everything/ Three Lectures,*[17] which is published here. The lectures "Suicide" and "Forced Annihilation" are included under the headings "On the Meaning and Value of Life" I and II, and the chapter on the concentration camps is now called "Experimentum Crucis." In these brief chapter headings, we can rediscover much about the thought and the fate of the author. First of all, the unconditional affirmation of life shines forth, which Frankl himself discusses in a letter from that time. In September 1945 he writes to his friends Wilhelm and Stepha Börner:

I am unspeakably tired, unspeakably sad, unspeakably lonely. . . . In the camp, you really believed you had reached the low point of life—and then, when you came back, you were forced to see that things had not lasted, everything that had sustained you had been destroyed, that at the time when you had become human again, you could sink even deeper into an even more bottomless suffering. Maybe there is nothing else left but to weep a little and to search through the Psalms. Maybe you will laugh at me, maybe you will be angry with me; but I do not contradict myself in the least; I take back nothing of my old affirmation of life when I experience the things I have described. On the contrary: if I had not had this rock-solid positive attitude to life, what would have become of me during these weeks, indeed those months in the concentration camp? But I see things in another dimension now. Increasingly, I realize that life is so infinitely meaningful that even in suffering and even in failure there still has to be a meaning.[18]

This deep respect for life always included the lives of others. As early as 1928, when still a medical student, Frankl had, with great personal commitment, set up youth counseling centers, which, above all, sought to prevent suicides among young people. Suicides became especially frequent at the time of year when school or college reports were issued; in fact, through the Report Action movement initiated by him, there was not a single student suicide in the summer of 1931. And even at that time he was convincingly describing the role of the meaning of life in connection with precautions against suicide:

For even if the spiritual causes of suicides are so different, the mental background is the lack of belief in a meaning to life. The person committing suicide not only lacks the courage to live, but also lacks humility before life. Only when a new morality replaces our new objectivity, only when the value of every human life is once again recognized as unique and incomparable, only then will mankind have the necessary mental hold to overcome spiritual crises.[19]

So again and again there is this belief in the meaning of life—even in the face of the suffering that is actually inherent in human life. The meaning of suffering was already laid out in a 1938 publication in which he spoke for the first time of the three categories of value: that is, creative, experiential, and attitudinal values.[20] But it is precisely the latter—the courageous and exemplary way of dealing with irremediable suffering—to which he attributes the highest rank. And so he says in the first part,

> Either we change our fate, if possible, or we willingly accept it, if necessary.

Such considerations were certainly not a mere academic game in those days, but a specific aid for living and surviving. Indeed, who had not suffered physical or spiritual damage from that great catastrophe? And Frankl himself—had he not lost everything that had been dear to him?

But he had found a way back into life, into a life that, in spite of everything, was still full of possibilities for meaning that needed to be realized. And with his publications and lectures he wanted to lead others to this way, to encourage them to find their own way out of the misery of the past years—even in the face of a still quite precarious present.

The title of the third part, "Experimentum Crucis,"
points to the fact that Frankl did not first develop his
ideas about the meaning of life as a resource in the concentration camp—as is sometimes reported. His book
Ärztliche Seelsorge (*The Doctor and the Soul*), in which
he had definitively formulated his theory on the human orientation toward meaning, had indeed existed in
manuscript form since 1941. In fact, he carried this manuscript with him during his deportation, still hoping that
he would be able to publish it one day. As he writes in his
memoirs, he eventually had to discard his coat with the
manuscript sewn in the lining.[21] In the camps, however,
he was able to observe that even in those extreme situ-
ations of the most bitter privation and profound degradation, all the ideas remained valid that he had already
perceived and systematically described in his work as a
youth counselor and psychiatrist. It turned out, in fact,
that those camp inmates who still recognized or at least
hoped for a meaning in life were the most likely to find
the strength to continue living, or finally to survive. Last
but not least, that was also true of himself: what kept
him alive was only the hope of seeing at least some of his
loved ones again and bringing the completed draft of his
book to publication.

In the summer of 1946, Frankl presented these insights, analyses, and encouragements to his audience in
his lectures—with rhetorical verve, scientific acuteness,
and the legitimation of someone who had experienced
the enduring value of his hypotheses in his own body,

his own soul. He published the most important and generally valid parts of the lecture cycle in book form in the same year. The numerous detailed discussions and reviews of this little book in newspapers, cultural and professional journals, and on the radio are a testament to how accurately he had hit the nerve of the time.[22]

—Franz Vesely,
Vienna, Summer 2019

ABOUT
VIKTOR E. FRANKL

Viktor E. Frankl was professor of neurology and psychiatry at the University of Vienna and, for twenty-five years, head of the Vienna Neurological Policlinic. The logotherapy and existential analysis he founded are also known as the "third Viennese direction of psychotherapy." He held visiting professorships at Harvard, Stanford, Southern Methodist, and Duquesne universities and was Distinguished Professor of Logotherapy at the US International University, San Diego, California. Frankl was born in Vienna in 1905. At the University of Vienna he gained a doctorate in medicine, later also a doctorate in philosophy. During the Second World War he spent three years in Auschwitz, Dachau, and other concentration camps. For four decades he made countless lecture tours all over the world. He received in total twenty-nine honorary doctorates from universities in Africa, Asia, Europe, and North and South America. He received numerous awards, including the Oskar Pfister Award from the American Psychiatric Association and honorary membership in the Austrian Academy of Sciences. Frankl's thirty-nine books have been published in fifty languages to date. The English version of *Trotzdem Ja zum Leben sagen (Man's Search for Meaning)* achieved sales in the millions and was included in the list of the "Ten most influential books in America" in a survey by the Library of Congress and the Book-of-the-Month Club. Viktor Frankl died in 1997 in Vienna.

FURTHER WORKS
BY VIKTOR E. FRANKL

A complete list of all books by Viktor Frankl and a comprehensive bibliography on logotherapy and existential analysis can be found on the website of the Viktor Frankl Institute: www.viktorfrankl.org.

ABOUT THE
VIKTOR FRANKL INSTITUTE

The Viktor Frankl Institute (VFI) was founded in Vienna in 1992 by an international circle of colleagues and friends under the aegis of Viktor Frankl. It is a scientific society with the goal of maintaining Viktor Frankl's work and promoting logotherapy and existential analysis as a psychiatric, psychological, and philosophical field of research and as applied psychotherapy. It is also responsible for quality assurance for psychotherapy and counseling training in logotherapy and existential analysis. The Viktor Frankl Institute in Vienna is also the accreditation institution for training in classical logotherapy and existential analysis (following Frankl).

A list of more than 150 accredited international institutions and national associations that provide training in logotherapy and existential analysis can be found on the VFI website.

The institute has exclusive access to the Viktor Frankl private archive and houses the world's largest collection of texts and research on logotherapy and existential analysis.

In 1999, in cooperation with the City of Vienna, the Viktor Frankl Fund of the City of Vienna was founded. In line with its objectives, each year, the fund awards prizes and scholarships to reward excellence and to promote research projects in the field of meaning-oriented humanistic psychotherapy. In addition, the fund awards an annual honorary prize in recognition and appreciation of the life's work of outstanding persons.

The institute offers the world's first state-accredited doctoral degree in logotherapy within the framework of the Viktor Frankl Chair of Philosophy and Psychology at the International Academy of Philosophy (University of the Principality of Liechtenstein). In collaboration with the Department for Logotherapy and Existential Analysis, founded in 2012 at the Graduate Institute of Psychoanalysis in Moscow, it also offers a master's program and psychotherapy training in logotherapy.

Information about the activities of logotherapy institutes around the world can be found on the homepage of the Viktor Frankl Institute, Vienna. In addition to news on logotherapeutic research and practice, it includes a comprehensive bibliography of primary and secondary literature on logotherapy.

Further information can be found at www.viktor frankl.org.

ABOUT DANIEL GOLEMAN
AND FRANZ VESELY

DANIEL GOLEMAN is an internationally known psychologist who lectures frequently to professional groups, business audiences, and on college campuses. As a science journalist, Goleman reported on the brain and behavioral sciences for the *New York Times* for many years. His 1995 book *Emotional Intelligence* has been a best-seller in many countries. Apart from his books on emotional intelligence, Goleman has written books on topics including self-deception, creativity, transparency, meditation, social and emotional learning, ecoliteracy, and the ecological crisis. He cofounded the Collaborative for Academic, Social, and Emotional Learning (www .CASEL.org) and also codirects the Consortium for Research on Emotional Intelligence in Organizations (www .eiconsortium.org) at Rutgers University.

DR. FRANZ VESELY is a university professor in physics. Since the death of his father-in-law, Viktor Frankl, he has managed Frankl's author's rights. As director of the Viktor Frankl Archive, he manages the representation of Frankl's extensive legacy. He is a cofounder and board member of the scientific society the Viktor Frankl Institute.

NOTES

1. Zyklon B (originally a pesticide) was the brand name of the highly poisonous hydrogen cyanide gas used by the Nazis for mass murder at Auschwitz and other death camps.

2. Bertolt Brecht (in collaboration with Kurt Weill), *The Threepenny Opera*, 1928.

3. Johann Wolfgang von Goethe (1749–1832), German author (Weimar Classicism), scientist, and statesman.

4. Friedrich Hölderlin (1770–1843), German Romantic poet and philosopher.

5. Christian Friedrich Hebbel (1813–1863), German poet and dramatist.

6. General paralysis is now known as tertiary syphilis or neurosyphilis. Penicillin was not yet used to cure syphilis in Austria in 1946, hence the reference to malarial therapy, which was still widely used.

7. Allusion to "O Herr, gib jedem seinen eigenen Tod . . ." ("Oh Lord, give to each his own death. . .") in Rainer Maria Rilke, *Das Stundenbuch* (*The Book of Hours*), 1905.

8. The early talkie *Atlantik* (1929), directed by E. A. Dupont, was based on a stage play about the *Titanic* disaster. English, French, and German versions were produced with different casts.

9. The author refers to the embattled Jewish population of Vienna following Kristallnacht (the November Pogroms) in 1938.

10. Ernst Kretschmer (1888–1964), German psychiatrist who categorized people by body build and linked these types to personality traits and mental illness.

11. "Cycloid personality," now known as cyclothymia, is a mood disorder similar to, but often milder than, bipolar disorder.

12. "Himmelhoch jauchzend, zum Tode betrübt" (rejoicing to high heaven, or in the depths of despair), from Goethe's play *Egmont* (1788), has become a common German saying.

13. Proverbs 13:12.

14. A conclusive experiment to prove that a particular hypothesis is true.

15. Viktor Frankl, *Gesammelte Werke, Band 1: Trotzdem Ja zum Leben sagen und ausgewählte Briefe (1945–1949)* [Collected works, vol. 1: Say yes to life in spite of everything and selected letters (1945–1949)], ed. A. Batthyany, K. H. Biller, E. Fizzotti (Vienna: Böhlau Verlag, 2005).

16. *Wiener Kurier*, March 23, 1946.

17. Viktor Frankl, *Trotzdem Ja zum Leben sagen/Drei Vorträge* [Say yes to life/Three lectures] (Vienna: Franz Deuticke, 1946).

18. Frankl, *Gesammelte Werke, Band 1*, 184.

19. "Workers' Day, April 14, 1934," in Gabriele Vesely-Frankl, ed., *Viktor E. Frankl: Frühe Schriften, 1923–1942* [Viktor E. Frankl: Early writings, 1923–1942] (Vienna: Maudrich, 2005).

20. V. E. Frankl, *Zur geistigen Problematik der Psychotherapie* [On the spiritual problem of psychotherapy],

Zentralblatt für Psychotherapie und ihre Grenzgebiete 10
(1938): 33–45.

21. Viktor Frankl, *Dem Leben Antwort geben: Autobi-
ografie* [Recollections: An autobiography] (Weinheim:
Beltz, 2017).

22. In the ten years after the book's publication, more
than thirty reviews were published in a variety of maga-
zines and newspapers in Austria, including the *Wiener Zei-
tung, Die Österreicherin,* and *Österreichische Ärztezeitung.*